Creati

for Jesus

The Glory of God
as declared by
the Dance of
Heaven and Earth

By James Lindemann

RFLindemann & Son, Publisher
2011

James (Jim) Lindemann

Webpage: lindespirit.com
email: jim@lindespirit.com
Blog: CovenantMusings.lindespirit.com

ISBN 978-0-9877280-1-2

Other titles by the author:
COVENANT: The Blood Is The Life
Celebration! - Holy Communion: A Love Story

RFLindemann & Son, Publisher
541 33 Street South
Lethbridge, Alberta, Canada T1J 3V7

RFL & Son, Publisher

ISBN 978-0-9877280-1-2

Flyleaf

Angels, men, stars and planets have taken their places. The Ballet is about to begin. But this is not merely about interesting heavenly movements, rather there is a story to be told. With the Bible pulling everything together, the Ballet takes shape. The constellations' themes hang as the backdrops; the festivals of the Jewish year give the troupe its depth, filling the stage with meaning. The times of gestation, circumcision, and purification make their presence felt. The "Blood Moon" adds its dramatic emphasis. Guided by the dance above them, based upon roots laid centuries before, the Magi make their journey in faith.

But ought we look, or is the Ballet forbidden to us? Are the heavens Satan's tool, or do they declare the Lord's Glory – and just what should we expect in regard to the Glory of God? This Ballet has much for its audience to think about.

The Author

The author, a pastor himself, is the recipient of perspectives, concerns and interests handed down from a long line of pastors in the Lutheran Church, hence his interest and background in such things as the Sacraments, the Covenant, and even the Star of Bethlehem. His Bible Study groups have also contributed greatly in developing these various themes, and now as retirement approaches, this is a good time to gather these thoughts into a more finished form.

Born and raised in New York City, he has come to also value the life in the smaller communities. With his deeply appreciated companion (his wife), their family bulges at the seams with four natural, two adopted, a variety of foster children, and now grandchildren – there is no end to the usually delightful competition for his attention. Perhaps in the coming years there may even be time to pursue his Master's interest in carpentry.

Acknowledgements

The first acknowledgement is to my father, whose interest in what that star was that Matthew wrote about also infected my curiosity. Also to the little Bible Study group in the Good Samaritan Society's Park Meadows assisted living residence in Lethbridge, Alberta, when they wanted to "do something for Christmas," it restarted my interest in the events surrounding the Birth of Jesus, which eventually led me to this book.

Two tools that were very handy in preparing this book are the program *Starry Night* (www.starrynight.com/) and the *Fourmilab Calendar Converter* (www.fourmilab.ch/documents/calendar/).

The *Calendar Converter* allows one to identify a date in its Gregorian, Julian, Hebrew, even Islamic, Persian, Mayan, Baha'i, Indian and other counterparts' notation. Of particular usefulness is the *Julian Day* calculation, where each date is given its number in a sequence starting from "Monday, 1st January of year 4713 B.C.E. in the Julian calendar" (where "B.C.E." is the same as "B.C." and "C.E." is the same as "A.D."). This allows determining the number of days within an interval a matter of simple subtraction, rather than having to count through each week and month. To operate the Converter, one simply enters the date or Julian Day number in its proper location, presses that location's "Calculate," and all the rest of the dates are changed to that day's relative value.

Mention should be made that the dates given in this study are in Julian, not in the modern Gregorian, format. The major difference, among others, is that the Latin numeral system had no "0," so in counting backwards, January 1, 1 AD, is preceded by December 31, 1 BC.

The *Starry Night* program is most useful. It allows one to view what happens in the heavens from any point (not just on earth but at least within the solar system) at any time within human history and its projected future. Much of what is in the section "The Ballet of the Sky" comes from watching what actually occurs in the sky at that time.

A note of gratefulness is extended to the enormous work that Ernest L Martin has done for his book *The Star that Astonished the World* (available in book form or free online: http://www.askelm.com/star/), which provides the opportunity to identify some elements in "The Ballet of the Sky." Also a word of thanks to Rick Larson (http://www.bethlehemstar.net) for planting ideas that ultimately added extra dance steps to the Ballet.

Table of Contents

Creation's Ballet for Jesus

The Glory of God as declared
by the Dance in Heaven and on Earth

By James Lindemann

I. The Prelude

> But when the fullness of the time had come, God sent forth His Son, born of a woman …
> Galatians 4:4-5

"When the time had fully come" – all is prepared: the political, the religious and even the heavenly spheres are all ready. It is humbling to realize how events are woven to create the setting for the most extraordinary phenomenon in the universe's history: God come into human flesh, Immanuel, "God is with us." Yet the path to this point is not easy. Indeed there are some terrible experiences, but the most frustrating of all is that for the 400 years before Jesus' birth, God is silent – there is no prophet in Israel! – a bewilderment captured, perhaps prophetically, in Psalm 74:9-10:

> We do not see our Covenant SIGNs; there is no longer a prophet, and not one among us knows for how long. For how long, O God, will the enemy taunt us? Shall the enemy scorn Your Name forever? Why do You withdraw *Your Hand – Your Right Hand?* Take it from Your bosom and destroy them!

Yet the Lord God *is* working, so that when it comes time to expose to all mankind His great Plan determined from before the universe's creation, the world would have the equipment to receive the best news humans ever have. And then the stars will dance.

II. Behind the Curtain: Getting the Props in Place

A. Foreign Rule

1. Persia (597- 538 BC)

"Behold, It Has Come... The End Has Come... Behold, It Has Come" *Ezekiel 7:5-6*

> I came to the captives at Tel Aviv ... I sat where they sat, and remained there being appalled among them seven days.   Ezekiel 3:15

Can one possibly fathom the anguish of soul that is reflected in Ezekiel's cry! After Solomon, the kingdom is split between the Northern Kingdom (Israel) and the Southern Kingdom (Judah). To discourage the North's people from coming to Jerusalem to worship, their first king, Jeroboam, sets up an alternate worship of golden calves [I Kings 12:26-29], a rebellion that eventually climaxes in the North's being carried off into captivity.

Unfortunately, the South does not learn from the North's fate, and therefore its own mixed spiritual loyalties cause it to also be led into captivity in Babylon. That God's People have come to this low point is almost incomprehensible to the prophets Isaiah, Jeremiah, and Ezekiel. Although they warn time and again of this impending doom, there is no way to imagine just how devastating it would be.

Persia is Sympathetic to Israel

Yet, the Chosen People are not even here abandoned. As the book of Daniel represents, individuals from this favored People achieve high positions within the conquering empire. And when Babylon is in turn defeated by Persia, this new ruling power also is not afraid to use the best, even from their conquered subjects. So Daniel is "chief governor over all the wise men of Babylon" [Daniel 2:48] and later "king [Darius] planned to appoint him over [all Persia]" [Daniel 6:3]; the book of Ezra opens with the declaration that God instructs King Cyrus to rebuild Jerusalem's temple and Ezra apparently is the king's liaison; so also Nehemiah is "Cupbearer" (prime minister?) to King Artaxerxes', who supports the rebuilding of Jerusalem's wall.

Preparing for the Gospel

"These neither snow nor rain nor heat nor darkness of night prevent from accomplishing each one his appointed task, with the very utmost speed" – although thought of as a motto by the United States Postal Service, these words first describe the Persian "Pony Express."[1] This mobility is made possible by an excellent interprovincial road system throughout the empire, along with a water link that stretches from the Indus River to the Red Sea. When it comes time to share the Good News of Jesus, these are important assets.

As will be identified later, Persia's main religion, Zoroastrianism with its monotheism (one God) and yet the dualism of "good and evil" with an evil personage, is very close to Judaism. How easily a sloppy theology could merge the two, yet one of the root reasons for the captivity is that Israel had never quite gotten rid of mixing other religions into their worship. The Jewish synagogues arise not only for worship of God, but to particularly focus on His written Word, which keeps in front of the People those places where God differs from what was all around them. As well, during this time the Scriptures is also translated into Aramaic (learned in Babylon), to which Nehemiah 8:8 may allude: "So they read from the Book, from the Torah of

God, rightly distinguishing to set out the sense, and helped them to understand the reading."

Through this background, the Magi are introduced to Israel's prophecies; and the People of the Promise develop a sense of identity: they truly are *GOD's* People and He is the only God.

2. Greece/Macedonia (333 – 323 BC)

Alexander: "Apostle of Hellenism"

In a short 33 years of lifetime, Alexander conquers a massive empire. But more than just preoccupied with victories, he takes along poets, city planners, anthropologists, biologists, musicians – having been tutored by Aristotle, he wants all his subjects to experience the benefits of the Greek culture. When a delegation of Jews shows him prophecies in Daniel that describe him, he agrees to spare Jerusalem, giving the Jews equal rights with the Greeks, and he even sacrifices to Jehovah. He founds Alexandria (Egypt) as a jewel of learning to usurp Babylon's dominance as a center of ancient life.

Preparing for the Gospel

The process of spreading the Greek culture to other nations is called "Hellenization," through which Alexander gives his empire a common everyday business language, which allows people to move freely from place to place and still be able to conduct business and even to discuss philosophy. This provides the language base best equipped to handle Christian spiritual concepts.

3. Egypt (Ptolemies) (323 – 204 BC)

Alexander's Broken Empire

Upon his death, Alexander's empire is split between his five generals. Greedy Antigonus (who has Asia Minor and Asia) is defeated as he tries to take more, and his territory is divided as Seleucus adds Syria and Asia Minor to his Babylon and Persia, and founds his new capital, *Antioch,* in honor of his father; meanwhile Ptolemy's territory reaches from Egypt to Palestine to Syria.

At first, life with the Ptolemies is very harsh: Jerusalem is sacked, thousands are exported to Alexandria, and tribute is demanded. The High Priest becomes an agent of a foreign power, and his nephew is appointed as a "tax farmer" (the precursor to the tax-collectors as agents of Gentile powers). Later, things are more relaxed: self-rule is allowed and religion is not interfered with.

Preparing for the Gospel

Due to the number of Jews in Egypt and North Africa, and because less of these Jews are able to read the Hebrew of the Old Testament, the Scriptures (the Old Testament) is translated into Greek as the *"Septuagint."* This gives the later Christian missionaries throughout the Roman Empire a common reference point for their teaching, from which St Paul quotes and which the Beroeans check in Acts 17:10-12.. Also, the translation in some parts seems to be especially Spirit-guided, for instance, Isaiah 7:14, in the Hebrew, giving birth to a son is a "young woman" who likely would be a virgin, but in the Greek, of all the words that could be chosen, the translators deliberately use "virgin" – making an unmistakable statement in regard to the understanding of the passage.

4. Syria (Seleucids) (198 - 164 BC)

Antiochus IV (175 – 164 BC)
– "Epiphanes" ("Illustrious One")
– or "Epimanes" ("Madman")

After being held for ransom in Rome for 13 years, Antiochus returns as an extreme Hellenist, eager to make the Jews "get on the bandwagon." Jerusalem is renamed as "New Antioch"; the Scriptures, the Sabbath, the Circumcision, the sacrifices are forbidden. The highest bribe gets the High Priest office, and Antiochus controls the temple treasury. There is extreme cruelty toward those refusing to convert to the Hellenic "culture."

The Hasidim, "Pious Ones," are formed in reaction to such mockery of their religion, but Antiochus knows the Jews and their vulnerability. In response to their rebellion, he mounts a savage *Sabbath* attack, since the Jews would not "work" – fight – on the holy day. Jerusalem's walls are leveled. In the temple is *"The Abomination of Desolation / Appalling Sacrilege"* that Jesus' listeners might recall [Matthew 24:15; Mark 13:14]: in this holy place, Antiochus' troops hold orgies to Bacchus; a statue of Zeus Dyonisius is installed; side rooms house cultic prostitutes for the Syrian soldiers; and swine is sacrificed on the altar, their blood sprinkled throughout the temple.

Meanwhile the Samaritans embrace Hellenization, disown their connection with the Jews, and rename their Mt Gerizim temple to honor Jupiter – this betrayal of their brothers in desperate need forms the backdrop to the animosity between the two groups during Jesus' time. Antiochus dies insane.

5. The Maccabees (164 - 67 BC)

Judas, "the Hammer," as a guerilla fighter is very successful against greater enemies and retakes Jerusalem. To rededicate and purify the temple, the decision is made to burn ritual oil in the Temple's menorah for eight days – but only one day's worth of oil is found. This oil is lit anyway and surprisingly it lasts the full eight days, which is the origin of *Hanukkah* ("Dedication") – the Festival of Lights. When he is defeated at Bethsura, Judas retreats to Jerusalem, which is besieged, but since Syria has problems elsewhere, peace with religious liberty is the outcome.

Brother Jonathan, taking the reins after Judas' assassination, seems to take a step backwards by playing politics. Supporting one contender to the Syrian throne, Jonathan manages to be named High Priest, governor, and Syrian noble – thereby mixing religious and political leaderships, which is against God's design to keep the two separate. He gets Rome to designate Judea as a "friend of Rome."

He is assassinated, and brother Simon takes up the cause again, by capturing Syrian strongholds, especially the citadel in Jerusalem. He wins independence for the Jews, home rule and tax exemption. He is proclaimed "Leader and High Priest forever," which begins the Hasmonean dynasty.

John Hyrcanus (135 - 104 BC) follows after Simon's assassination, conceding Joppa and coastal cities to Syria in a mutual defense pact, and destroying the Samaritan Mt Gerizim Temple. Alexander Jannaeus/Jonathan (103 – 76 BC), son of Aristobulus (Rome's designated "King" of the Jews), expands control to a size that rivals Solomon's empire. Herod's father, Antipater, governor of Idumea, appears at this time.

Salome Alexandra (76 – 67 BC) takes over the reins next. She reconciles with the Pharisees, which are the offspring of the Hassidim, who have been alienated both by the mixing of the political and the religious leaderships, as well as by the courtships of Syria and Rome. Her brother Simeon ben Shetah, president of Sanhedrin, introduces elementary education for boys in

Synagogue schools. However, sadly, her sons bring civil war (one side being supported by Antipater) and Rome enters to resolve the conflict.

6. Rome (63 BC – to NT times)

Jewish rebel troops force Pompey to siege Jerusalem, however he prevents looting and burning once he gains entrance. Still, Rome is bewildered by the Jews whose religion is nothing like any other nation's. For example, Pompey is curious since he sees no statues or idols depicting their God. Finally, to the horror of the Jews, determined to see what they do worship, he forces his way into the temple's *Holy of Holies*, the one room that even the High Priest could enter only once a year on *Yom Kippur ("the Day of Atonement")*. Since *the Ark of the Covenant* was lost either when Egypt carted off "the treasures of the temple" [II Chronicles 12:9] or at the destruction of the first temple by Babylon [II Kings 25 and II Chronicles 36:18, although *the Ark* is not mentioned], the room now is absolutely empty, prompting Pompey to claim that the Jews must be atheists.

Judea is made part of Rome's Syrian province, Samaria and Decapolis become independent of Judea. The Hasmonean, Hyrcanus, remains High Priest and is made Ethnarc of Judea and Perea

B. The Rise of the Religious/Political Parties

The *Hasidim*, formed in reaction to Antiochus IV's atrocities, reject the power-hungry and corrupt Maccabees and consider the combining of political and priestly powers as sacrilege. The *Pharisees (Perushim* – "Separated Ones") are their offspring, holding to the spiritual values of their heritage; they believe in: 1) the spirit world (angels and demons); 2) the reality of the soul and immortality; 3) the bodily resurrection; and 4) the judgment to come. However, they go beyond Scripture, they add "new Festivals

(*Chanukah* [*Hanukkah*] and *Purim*) … they added to the canon of Scripture … they added new doctrine … [and] new rites to the Temple worship …"[2]

Hasidim ascetic purists become the *Essenes*, who condemn "the wicked priest" (probably Alexander Jannaeus, who apparently is very cruel), and who desire true worship of God. Their persecuted "Teacher of Righteousness," perhaps a High Priest or some coming prophet, is unknown and does not quite fit John the Baptist nor Jesus.

The *Scribes*, who already gained prominence in Ezra and Nehemiah, become more established and by nature of their craft become theological lawyers who are sympathetic to the Pharisees.

Many priests are Hellenists (Greek culture), therefore rationalists and Skeptics, and are the *Sadducees*. In favor of the Hellenistic free will of man, they reject predestination; being thorough-going philosophical materialists, they reject the spirit world, along with the immortal soul and resurrection [Acts 23:8], which can be a puzzle since as priests this is their realm.

The *Zealots* do not stand for any heathens, whether a country or an individual, having ultimate rule over God's Chosen People. As the terrorists of their day, to them human life is cheap and any death could be rationalized into supporting their cause. They look forward to a Messiah that will lead a revolt from Rome and will reestablish the throne of David. Jesus' disciple, Simon [Luke 6:15; Acts 1:13] is a Zealot, and possibly Judas Iscariot is a sympathizer as well.

Indeed, there is an undercurrent of expectation: the historians, Suetonius, Tacitus, Josephus all report on a rumor that a world leader is coming from Palestine.[3] Jona Lendering adds:

> Some Jewish scholars had discovered that seventy-six generations had passed since the Creation, and there was a well-known prophecy that the

Messiah was to deliver Israel from its foreign rulers in the seventy-seventh generation.[4]

Even in Persia, there is the anticipation that "the stock of Abraham" would bring forth "a king who would raise the dead and transform the world into a kingdom of peace and security."[5] The Pharisees believe that their Messiah would descend to the center of Temple courtyard (which apparently forms the basis of one of Jesus' temptations [Matthew 4:5-7, Luke 4:9-12]). Rabbi Gamaliel, in Acts 5:35-39, describes the heightened expectations by giving a few examples of individuals who thought themselves as God's answer to the Jews, only to be killed and their followers scattered.

C. The Stage is Set

In the *Pax Romana*, an unusual peace and justice covers the Roman world. There is ease of travel throughout the Roman and the old Persian empires: the Mediterranean Sea is clear of pirates, and Roman troops keep robbers at bay on land; a widespread commercial language, *Koine* Greek, also lends itself better suited to the philosophical and spiritual demands of the spread of Christianity than Latin does.

Through the *Diaspora* ("Scattering") of the Jews, the synagogue and the availability of God's Word in understandable common languages (the Greek *Septuagint* and the Arabic translations) is in place in Europe, Africa, Asia Minor and southwest Asia. The prophecies stand ready, for example, Isaiah 7:14's prophecy of the virgin, and Daniel's prophecy of the timing of the Messiah.

The tension between the Samaritans and the Jews is ready to form the backdrop of various incidents in Jesus' life. The Pharisees, the Scribes, the Sadducees and others have taken their positions. The hardships of the Jews have forced appreciation and need for God's action.

The House of Magi from the East sees the heavens beginning their series of special events.

All is indeed ready.

III. To You is Born

A. The Curtain Rises

1. A Prophet Stands in the Wings

After a long 400 years of "silence," God speaks. In Luke 1:11-17, the angel Gabriel appears to the priest Zachariah who is performing his official duties in the temple. The message is that a child is to be born of a couple "as good as dead" – too old to have children. This will be a special child for a special mission: "John" will be his name, and he will prepare the way for the long-awaited Messiah.

2. God Makes His Move To Humanity

Again God speaks, again through the angel Gabriel, to Mary [Luke 1:28-35]. The news is almost impossible to fathom: by the power of the Holy Spirit she will conceive and bear a Son, Jesus, the Son of God.

3. The Family is Ready

Jesus is to grow up in a family, because this is the way God provides love, care, and security for a child. Mary also is to be protected from observers that might accuse her of adultery. God speaks yet again [Matthew 1:18-25], and Joseph is brought into this select group.

4. Places, Everyone! – The World is Moved

The Commonly-Used Time Frame

In Luke 2:1-7, a census is taken of the Roman Empire and moves "the world" all around, particularly Mary and Joseph to Bethlehem, the prophetic birthplace of the Messiah. But what and when is this census? Herod's death plays a key role here in establishing a time frame. Rome's Jewish historian, Flavius Josephus, tells us that Herod dies after a lunar eclipse[6] – there is a lunar eclipse on March 13, 4 BC –, and it appears that he stops reigning after 4 BC. And there is a taxation/census in 8 BC[7], which therefore seems to settle the matter.

But it is not that easy. Attempts to establish the approximate time of Jesus' birth have floundered, with conjectures anywhere from 12 BC to 5 BC. Ancient Christian writers and other sources who indicate a birth closer to 1 BC are ignored with the attitude that they are obviously mistaken. Although this present book will not comprehensively survey all the reasons why the date of Herod's death can and should be re-evaluated, it is hoped that the following will at least open the door. This in turn allows the heavens in 3-2 BC to tell their story in regard to the most amazing event to which the universe has ever been witness: the coming of God the Son into the flesh.

The Better Census

The taxation of 8 BC[8] at best might affect Joseph "as a male and thus presumably a property-owner,"[9] but does it require a woman (the now *very* pregnant Mary), who in those days is unlikely to own property, to make the journey to Bethlehem? It is doubtful. In fact, as a land-owner in Nazareth, it is more reasonable that Joseph would be taxed at Nazareth, rather than in

"David's town." As well, that taxation must really be stretched to make it last until Jesus' birth.[10]

However, on February 5, 2 BC, the Senate and the people of Rome confer on Caesar Augustus the title *Pater Patriae* ("Father of the 'Fatherland'"), on the occasion of his 25th anniversary as emperor, which coincides with the 750th anniversary of the "founding" of Rome.[11] At this occasion he is presented with the results of a census that has been combined with an oath of allegiance, taken of all the peoples of the whole empire.[12]

> Orosius (a fifth century historian) clearly links an oath to the registration at the birth of Christ:
> "[Augustus] ordered that a census be taken of each province everywhere and that all men be enrolled. So at that time, Christ was born and was entered on the Roman census list as soon as he was born. This is the earliest and most famous public acknowledgment which marked Caesar as the first of all men and the Romans as lords of the world ... that first and greatest census was taken, since in this one name of Caesar all the peoples of the great nations took oath, and at the same time, through the participation in the census, were made part of one society." [Orosius, *Adv. Pag.* VI.22.7, VII.2.16; trans. by Deferrari, R.J. *The Fathers of the Church* (Washington, D.C.: Catholic U. Press, 1964), vol. 50, p. 281, 287]. He identified the time of the census using two Roman systems that both agree to indicate 2 B.C. [A.U.C. 752 = Augustus' 42nd year = 2 B.C. (*Adv. Pag.* VI.22.1, VI.22.5, VII.2.14)].   John P. Pratt[13]

Josephus[14] writes that "all the people of the Jews gave assurance of their good will to Caesar, and to the king's government." However, Herod is in a situation where he is in disgrace before Augustus, so a group of 6,000 Pharisees, seizing the opportunity to embarrass him, "refuse to swear the oath" and are fined. Since this census was ordered in 3 BC, Herod had to still be alive to experience this revolt. Pursiful adds "It certainly would not have helped his mood should visitors from the east bring word of one 'born king of the Jews' some time shortly thereafter."[15]

This census likely does involve *both* Joseph *and* Mary, since both are of royal lineage and either one could bring forth a potential contender to the Jewish throne, therefore they would pledge themselves and their offspring in fealty to Caesar. But does a census really move people around? Pursiful points out that an Egyptian provincial census decree from 104 AD compels people to return to their hometowns to be registered:

> Gaius Vivius Maximus, Prefect of Egypt [says]: seeing that the time has come for the house to house census, it is necessary to compel all those who for any cause whatsoever are residing out of their provinces to return to their own homes, that they may both carry out the regular order of the census and may attend diligently to the cultivation of their allotments.[16]

Pursiful also mentions that Justin Martyr (*First Apol.* 1:34), Tertullian (*Adv. Marc.* 4:7), Cyril of Jerusalem and other ancient writers appeal to now no longer available census records where Jesus is entered in the rolls, however such records are dismissed out-of-hand as merely "probable forgeries."[17]

John the Baptist

> In the fifteenth year of the reign of Tiberius Caesar, Pontius Pilate being governor of Judea, Herod being tetrarch of Galilee, his brother Philip tetrarch of Iturea and of the region of Trachonitis, and Lysanias tetrarch of Abilene, in the high priesthood of Annas and Caiaphas, the word of God came to John the son of Zacharias in the wilderness.   Luke 3:1-2

"Now, in the fifteenth year" seems pretty straightforward, and probably Luke means it that way, but – well…, it is just discouraging for a layman. Basically, John the Baptist begins his career in the fifteenth year of Tiberius; when Jesus begins his ministry after His baptism, *He* is "*about* 30 years old" [Luke 3:23]. Note that John's age is not given, only Jesus'. Although the traditional age of spiritual maturity is 30 years old – hence Jesus begins His ministry at about that age –, a "prophet" tends to be in a different class: "But Jehovah said to me, 'Do not say, "I am a child"; for to all whom I send you you shall go, and all which I command you you shall speak'" [Jeremiah 1:7]. Even "the child" Samuel is called to be a prophet (I Samuel 2:18, 21, 26; 3:1). So "the fifteenth year" of Tiberius' reign does not necessarily speak to the age of John, only as to when he begins his ministry.

From the descriptions in the Gospels, how much time transpires for John to be established as the new Elijah who is "preparing the way"? How much leeway on either side does Jesus' age's "about" encompass, six months (their age difference), ten months? Still, counting back from this point ought to give us some sort of ballpark for a general limit.

The *real* problem occurs as to when Tiberius' reign starts. On July 1, 12 AD, Tiberus begins ruling jointly with the aged Augustus. In the third year of this joint rule, Augustus dies on August 19, 14 AD and Tiberius is the official new Caesar on September 17 of that year. A problem comes in regard to how the Jews and others count time, since they count the present fragment of the time unit as 1. Hence, a week from today, which *we* call the seventh day, to the Jews, who count the fragment of today as the first day, it is the *eighth* day.

So, is Luke counting the first year of when Augustus and Tiberius *jointly* rule as year 1, or, in addressing the Greco-Roman world, does he count it as "0" (the "accession" year) and the next year as year 1? Or perhaps he is starting when Tiberius alone ruled – again, is the first year "1" or is it "0"?[18] The website: "star.wind.mystarband.net"[19] offers this table:

TABLE 150. *Regnal Years of Tiberius Caesar*

A.U.C.	AD		Col 1	Col 2	Col 3	Col 4
765	12	Tiberius governs jointly with Augustus	1			
766	13		2	1		
767	14	Aug 19, death of Augustus. Sept 17,	3	2	1	

		Tiberius named head of state				
768	15		4	3	2	1
769	16		5	4	3	2
779	26		15	14	13	12
780	27		16	15	14	13
781	28		17	16	15	14
782	29		18	17	16	15

Anno Urbis Conditae (A.U.C.) comes from *Ab urbe condita*, Latin for "from the founding of the City (Rome)", and is *traditionally* set in 753 BC.

It is important to remember that "the fifteenth year of Tiberius" is in regard to John the Baptist, not Jesus. We do not know how long it takes for John to become established. Possibly Jesus is baptized within the same year, or possibly some subsequent year. Therefore, Jesus is born around 1 BC – no wait, perhaps it is 2 BC, or is it 3 or 4 BC? Still, the general outcome is that there is good reason to find the birth of Jesus at a date closer toward, for example, 1 BC than 5 BC and earlier.

Backwards from the Crucifixion

Another possible tool is to determine the date of the crucifixion. The Gospel of John indicates that at least two *Passovers* occur within Jesus' ministry, in John 2 and 6, and He is crucified at the third, John 11ff. On this basis, his ministry encompasses at least 2-3 years. Allowing "about" 3 years to be added to the "about 30" in the material above, we have "about" 33 years for Jesus' age at death.

The task will be to determine *the Passover* at which Jesus dies. There are two days identified in the Gospels: the first is the Day of Unleavened Bread, the Day of Preparation on which the *Passover* lambs are killed [Mat 26:17; Mark 14:12; Luke 22:7]; it also is the day on which Jesus dies and is buried [Luke 23:53, 54 John 19:41-42]. The day that follows is *the Passover* itself, which is also "the Sabbath" [Mark 15:42; Luke 23:54]. According to the *Fourmilab Calendar Converter,* the only year in which *Nissan* 15 (*Passover*) occurs on a Saturday in the 30 AD neighborhood is 33 AD. In 30 AD itself, *Nissan* 15 is calculated to be on a Thursday (although *Starry Night* indicates the full moon the next night), the other years are calculated as even earlier in the week.

So *Passover*, 33 AD minus a "hard" 33 years would indicate spring of 1 BC as the approximate birth time of Jesus (keeping in mind that there is no year "0"). It seems that a "fudge" principle is needed, since the nearest candidate for the "census" is the census/oath of allegiance in 3-2 BC. Perhaps the census is not quite over by February 5, 2 BC and does continue on for a few months; meanwhile a leeway of months in regard to Jesus' "about 30" would also need to be to be employed – a bit of a stretch, but it could work.[20]

Phlegon

If one counts by Olympiads, the four year (summer to summer) units based on the Olympic games, Phlegon (2nd century AD) writes about the events believed to surround Jesus' death:

> However in the fourth year of the 202nd olympiad, an eclipse of the sun happened, greater and more excellent than any that had happened before it; at the sixth hour, day turned into dark night, so that the stars were seen in the sky, and an earthquake in Bithynia toppled many buildings of the city of Nicaea.[21]

202 times 4 equals 808 years, minus 776-775 BC (thought to be the first year of the first Olympiad) yields 32-33 AD.[22] Again subtracting 33 years, Jesus' birth would occur in 2-1 BC.

Ancient Authorities

Various ancient church fathers seem to indicate that Jesus is born around 2 BC and that Herod dies in 1 BC.[23] They are often discounted, mostly it seems because they do not agree with modern historians – after all, the "fathers" are regarded as too far removed in time (some by a whole century and a half and at least two generations!) and could not be very careful investigators – this is in contrast to the 20-century-removed modern historians who can only conjecture the date and are often in disagreement! On the contrary, the "fathers" are likely to be far more comfortable with the dating processes of the time and likely have access to documents and information no longer in existence.

Josephus, apparently regarded as the superior authority (although himself is at least second generation to the events that happened almost a 100 years earlier), has his problems, for example, when he writes that Herod dies at about age 70, and yet was appointed governor of Galilee at age 15 in 47 BC – this means the king dies in 8 AD (70 minus [15 plus 47] equals 8 AD), which is much too late. Yet if the 47 BC age is *adjusted* to 25, then it confirms that Herod dies about 2-1 BC.[24]

Other Eclipse Candidates[25] and the "Blood Moon"

If Josephus refers to the March 13, 4 BC or an earlier eclipse as to when Herod dies, then he appears to contradict himself, according to the last paragraph. If the Census/Oath of Allegiance of 3-2 BC is indeed the better choice for the circumstances surrounding Jesus' birth, it would require a later eclipse.

The 4 BC eclipse occurs just as morning is breaking and therefore is larger and more noticeable in the sky – but does it raise eyebrows enough as compared with a total, blood-red eclipse, which happens on January 10, 1 BC (*Shevat* 15)? (A "Blood Moon" occurs because the edge of the earth acts like a prism, bending the colors of light; the long red spectrum bends most, and the Moon is at just the right distance to therefore be illuminated with a deep red hue.) Certainly this eclipse would be a fitting, celestially ironic, description to the end of the bloody reign of Herod. However, it begins about 2 AM, reaching totality about 3:30 AM; the Moon begins to emerge at about 6 AM and sets at about 7:30 AM – so only very early risers would see it. And as we will see, it may have other implications.

There is also an eclipse on December 29, 1 BC (*Teveth* 13), which in about a half hour after the Sun sets and the Moon rises, at about 6:15 PM, the earth's shadow begins to cover the large Moon. By about 8 PM coverage is as far as it will go, about 58%, and the eclipse is over at about 10 PM – an event quite visible to the population.[26]

The Scroll of Fasts

The Megillat Taanit [Scroll of Fasts] is a very early (first century A.D.) list of memorable days in Jewish history, which were kept as special days in the calendar, when fasting was not permitted. Most of the entries in it refer to events which happened between the second century B.C. and the first century A.D. They are arranged in twelve sections, according to the Jewish month in which they occurred.[27]

There are two entries of interest:

On the 7th thereof [of *Kislev*] (a holiday).

On the 7th[28] of *Shebat* [*Shevat*] is a holiday, whereon it is not allowed to mourn.

Only for these two days are no reasons given as to why there are to be no fasts – possibly for the sake of political prudence. Herod knows that the Jews would never mourn his passing, so as he realizes death is immanent, he calls together all the elders of Judah, then locks them in the hippodrome with orders to have them killed the moment he dies – therefore there will be mourning at his death, even if it is not for him. The sentence is never carried out. It is reasonable that the Jews would not just celebrate his death, but in rebuttal to his intent, would also refuse to have *any* mourning *ever* on this date, which suggests the *Shevat* 7[29] date, although some prefer *Kislev* 7.[30]

However, now with Herod's sons ruling the territory, and son Archelaus (ruler of Judea) apparently of similar nature to his father (this is why Joseph, upon returning from Egypt, decides to return to Nazareth rather than to Bethlehem [Matthew 2:22; Luke 2:39]), it probably is wiser to not *announce* the purpose of the celebration, hence no reason for the "holiday" is given.

Since Herod dies after an eclipse: in 1 BC, *Shevat* 7 occurs on January 2[31] – too early for the January 10 (*Shevat* 15) total eclipse. *Kislev* 7 occurs on Nov 23, ten months later and one month before the December 29, (*Teveth* 13) eclipse. After the December 29, 1 BC eclipse, now in 1 AD, *Shevat* 7 occurs twenty-three days later on January 21, and *Kislev* 7 occurs 11 months later on Nov 12. This favors the December 29, 1 BC eclipse and *Shevat* 7 on January 21, 1 AD as the date of Herod's death.[32]

More Tiberius Dating

6. About this time it was that Philip, Herod's brother, departed this life, in the twentieth year of the reign of Tiberius, after he had been tetrarch of Trachonitis and Gaulanitis, and of the nation of the Bataneans also, thirty-seven years.   Josephus[33]

Researchers have found that in regard to this passage from Josephus, almost all the copies printed before 1544 have the text "the twenty-second year of Tiberius."[34] Moving Philip's reign to two years later moves Herod's death two years later (also consider the confusion noted above about when Tiberius' reign "begins"):

It was also found that the oldest versions of the text give variant lengths of reign for Philip of 32 and 36 years. But if we still allow for a full thirty-seven year reign, then "the twenty-second year of Tiberius" (A.D. 35/36) points to 1 B.C. (1 year B.C. + 36 years A.D. = 37 years) as the year of death of Herod. This is therefore the date which is accepted in the present book. Accordingly, if the birth of Jesus was two years or less before the death of Herod in 1 B.C., the date of the birth was in 3 or 2 B.C., so consistently attested by the most credible early church fathers.   Jack Finegan[35]

Dating Herod

Murrell Selden figures the date of Herod's death this way: [36]

Establishing the Regnal Years for Herod the Great

My anchor for dating the regnal years for Herod the Great is a well known date, the battle for the Roman Empire at Actium. At this time there was a major earthquake, and it was in the life of Josephus. Here is what Josephus tells us at page 320, Book XV, Chapter V, Section 2, as follows: "2. At this time it was that the fight happened at Actium, between Octavius Caesar and Anthony in the seventh year of the reign of Herod; and then it was also that there was as earthquake in Judea, such a one as had not happened at any other time...."

Roman history tells us that the date of the decisive battle was September 2nd of 31 B. C. … In any case, it is a very firm anchor date from secular history. Elsewhere in Josephus, there is a narrative of how Herod had come to the aid of Mark Antony in the Spring of 31 B. C.

Table on the Reign of Herod

Year, B. C.		Regnal Years Period	
37		1	
36		2	
…			
32		6	
31	**war at Actium**	**7**	**anchor year**
30		8	
…			
18		20	
17	Herod began temple	21	
16		22	
…			
5		33	
4 B. C.		34	**the common error**
3		35	
2		36	
1 B. C.	**Herod died**	**37**	**since king by Rome**
did not reign - dead		38	died last year

23

Is this table correct? This writer believes it is correct, in reference to the time when the Romans appointed Herod as king. Observe please this statement from Book XVII, Chapter VIII, Section 1, by Josephus as follows:

"When he had done those things, he died the fifth day after he had caused Antipater to be slain; having reigned, since he procured Antigonus to be slain, thirty-four years; but since he had been declared king by the Romans, thirty-seven."

Ernest Martin identifies many places where Josephus has problems, particularly when Herod is pronounced King of the Jews by the Roman senate:

This does not end Josephus' chronological anomalies. He tells us that Herod's appointment as king was in the 184th Olympiad which was inaccurate by a few months with his next reference which said it took place when Calvinus and Pollio were consuls (40 B.C.E.). However, a close inspection of what Josephus stated, and comparing it with other Roman records, we find that Herod was actually made king in the spring of 38 B.C.E. (not in 40 B.C.E.). That is not all. Cassius Dio said Herod captured Jerusalem in 38 B.C.E., while some scholars think Josephus identified its capitulation with the year of 37 B.C.E. in the first part of a sentence and in the latter part of the same sentence Josephus indicates it was in 36 B.C.E. These contradictions have given modern historians considerable difficulty in arriving at chronological exactitudes from Josephus.   Martin[37]

There are also anomalies in Josephus' treatment of Herod's reign. In the first years of Herod's kingship, he buttressed his history with known and reliable chronological eras of time. He equated Herod's seventh year with the year following the Battle of Actium. Josephus also gave reference to the Olympiads (a reasonably known international chronological benchmark). Josephus continued giving such exact dates until Herod's twenty-eighth year (a few years before the birth of Jesus). But from then on, for some unexplained reason, Josephus stopped giving chronological indications which would link the latter years of Herod's reign with known historical eras. He did not resume his normal international cross-references until the tenth year of Archelaus (son of Herod) in C.E. 6. From then until the Jewish War of C.E. 66 to 73 his chronological references are sensible.

Why did Josephus abandon internationally recognized chronological references from 9 B.C.E. to C.E. 6? No one knows. But this very period of time is when Roman historians are sadly saddled with deficient chronological evidence for what was happening in the Roman Empire. Some of the most important events in Palestinian and Roman history occurred during that period of sixteen years. But for all those years, not one historical event mentioned by Josephus is cross-referenced to the Olympiads, the Battle of Actium, the years of the Roman consuls, or to the year of Caesar's reign.

These and other factors have caused historians to suspect the motives of Josephus in his writings of history. The German scholar Stauffer has summed up some of the problems in accepting Josephus without a critical eye.

"The past fifty years of research on the work of Josephus have taught us to be severely critical of his method and presentation. Josephus had an ax to grind. His historical journalism was intended as a self-defense and self-aggrandizement. He wrote to glorify his people and to eulogize the Roman Emperor. He was an ardent sympathizer with the pro-Roman collaborationists among the Jews and an opponent of all the anti-Roman and anti-Herodian partisans of the Palestinian resistance movement. Crucial parts of Josephus' historical works, moreover, were casually patched together from older sources of uneven value: consequently they were replete with gaps and contradictions, are muddled and misleading. This is particularly true of his remarks on Augustus, Herod, Quirinius, and the census. Of course, Josephus remains an invaluable source: but he is not to be read uncritically."   Martin[38]

Bewilderment

Ernest Martin, in his book, particularly in chapters 7 and following, does a very good job of describing the chaos that surrounds dates during the time period around which Jesus is born. There are ample discussions by other modern commentators in regard to how Quirinius/Cyrenius fits – or does not fit – into the picture, and also Saturnius, and Varus, and on, and on.

It has been thought that the discovery of coins with dates should be a reliable source. But when a coin says year 7 of someone's reign, the problem is in how one counts the beginning of his reign, especially if there are co-regencies involved. Herod himself counts his rule from the Roman Senate's proclamation, even though someone else actually sits on the throne until Herod conquers Jerusalem over three years later. It all depends on when and how you start the numbering system.

Reasons can be found why Herod's three sons who followed him might claim more years than they really ruled. One reason is a co-regency of some kind. There is some support for this in Josephus. Another reason is that the actual royal Hasmonean dynasty princes died several years before Herod's death. Claiming fictional years back to the royal sons would mean there was no intervening ruler who deserved the throne. An additional reason might be to claim years first designated for Herod's son Antipater to be king in Herod's will. After Herod discovered that Antipater was plotting against him, Herod's will was changed and Antipater was executed. Now the discovery of an old, original reading in the earliest manuscripts of Josephus gives new evidence that Herod Phillip began his reign in 1BC and not 4 BC. The discovery of a coin with a date that pushes another son's rule even earlier than 4 BC casts still more doubt on the reliability of coin dating in general, and on 4 BC as Herod's death year in particular.[39]

Ultimately, it is recognized that the reader will come to his own conclusions, and although no matter what date or date system one chooses, it will be challenged and no challenge nor defense will be definitive. However, there is good reason to open up the years between 3 to 1 BC as part of this book's consideration and let what is displayed in the skies over Bethlehem also have *its* say. Therefore this seemingly eternal rounds of discussion to pinpoint an indisputable date for, for instance, Herod's death is left for others much more versed in history.[40]

B. Bethlehem

1. The Scene at the Stable – Luke 2:4-7

Joseph also went up from Galilee, out of the city of Nazareth, into Judea, to the city of David, which is called Bethlehem, because he was of the house and family of David, to be registered with Mary, who was

26

betrothed to him and who was pregnant. And it happened that while there, the days of her pregnancy were fulfilled, and she gave birth to her Son, the Firstborn. She wrapped Him in swaddling cloths, and laid Him in a manger, because there was not a place for them in the inn.

Some writers believe that Jesus' birth coincides with one of the three major festivals where "all your males shall appear before the LORD your God at the place which he chose: at the Feast of Unleavened Bread, at the Feast of Weeks, and at the Feast of Booths" [Deuteronomy 16:16]. With such a huge number of people converging on Jerusalem, a "bedroom" community such as Bethlehem, six miles away, might experience some of the overflow, hence the full inn. So also, if it is a major festival, Mary might go along because, as the spiritual person she is, she enjoys attending these important highlights of her faith.

The difficulty here is that there is not a word about such a connection to a festival mentioned in the Bible, not by Matthew who is very Jewish-environment conscious, nor by Luke the precise researcher, nor by John who is very symbolism conscious. And that the very pregnant Mary, almost to deliver, with labor pains and the rest of the discomfort, with no landing spot when she arrives, with no familiar friends or midwives surrounding her – it is awkward to assume that she would merely tag along for the sake of a festival that is yearly, if she really does not have to.

Equally so, would not the Romans deliberately avoid the festivals for the sake of logistics? It is reasonable, considering what a counting nightmare it would be to weed through the additional 2 to 3 million extra people in Jerusalem during these times. On the other hand, assuming that Luke is indeed referring to the oath-of-allegiance census, and such an empire-wide counting takes months, the driving force may be to get as much done before Augustus' "Pater Patriae" celebration as possible despite the festivals, although probably still halting for the Sabbaths and major celebrations.

Actually, Luke does not bother and does not need to explain why the inn is full. Who knows, maybe the ancient version of the Shriners – at that time, all six of them? – are having their convention during this week. Inns, especially in such a small town which probably has only one, likely do not have many rooms. How many travelers and/or caravans who just happen to be passing through can fill them up? Simply, the inn is full.

2. The Scene in the Fields – Luke 2:8-20

Shepherds were in the same country, living in the fields, keeping guard over their flock in the night. An angel of the Lord stood before them, and the Glory of the Lord shone around them, and they were terribly afraid. The angel said to them, "Do not fear, for behold, I announce to you good news of great joy which will be to all people; because born to you this day in the city of David a Savior, Who is Christ the Lord. This is the sign to you: You will find a Baby wrapped in swaddling cloths, lying in a manger."

Suddenly there was with the angel a multitude of the heavenly host praising God and saying: "Glory in the highest to God, and on earth peace, goodwill toward men!"

So it was, as the angels departed from them into heaven, the shepherds said to one another, "Let us now go to Bethlehem and see this word that has happened, which the Lord has made known to us." So they went with haste and searched out both Mary and Joseph, and the Baby Who was lying in the manger. When they saw this, they made public the word spoken to them concerning this Child; and all who heard marveled at what the shepherds told them.

But Mary preserved all these words and pondered them in her heart.

The shepherds returned, glorifying and praising God for all they had heard and seen, as it had been told them.

Is there is a clue here about the time of year? As usual, there is no definite solution. It seems to be a common practice that the sheep would not be out in the field at night during the cold winter rainy months, which would rule out, as an example, a December 25 birth date.[41] However (here we go again),

In fact, the Mishnah (Shekalim 7:4) deals with the possibility of flocks being kept in the fields near Bethlehem, even in winter. This was the rainy season in Judea, when green grass was abundant. Although chilly, the nighttime lows would not be oppressively cold. Televised coverage of Christmas midnight mass from Bethlehem commonly shows worshipers in shirtsleeves.   Darrell Pursiful[42]

C. Visitors From the East

1. Magi

Magi (Greek *Magos*) is derived from the Persian word *Magus,* equal to the Hebrew *chakam,* meaning "having great intelligence, wisdom and prudence." They are one of the six major "houses" of Persia, a hereditary scientist-priest caste of the Medes (known today as the Kurds)[43], widely respected[44], the repository of Persian religious lore and learning[45], and religiously are comparable to the Levites and to Aaron's descendents in Israel. The Jewish philosopher Philo, a contemporary of Jesus, writes:

> Among the Persians there is a body of the Magi, who, investigating the works of nature for the purpose of becoming acquainted with the truth, do at their leisure become initiated themselves and initiate others in the divine virtues by very clear explanations.[46]

During the Parthian Dynasty, Persia is ruled through a King and the Megistanes (related to "*magi*strate" and roughly equivalent to a Parliament) plus advisers. The Megistanes' Lower House are the "Sophoi" or "Wise Ones," while the Upper House are the "Magoi" or "Great Ones," who give civil and political counsel with religious authority, since knowledge of the heavens and the configurations of heavenly bodies, along with various other scientific pursuits, are their occupation. Although one might think of them as the king-makers in the Persian Empire, their failed brief revolt around 520

BC[47] ends with Darius becoming king and their power is somewhat demoted.

2. Zoroaster/Zarathustra

Zoroaster is the "wise prophet" of the religion that bears his name, which apparently forms the basis of the Magian belief structure. He emphasizes diplomatic skill and logical thinking; he avoids the fantastic, accenting rather the practical, tangible and concrete; the theology is a clearly conceived plan and stands on a high moral level.

All other gods are demoted, which leaves only one uncreated Creator God, *Ahura Mazda* ("the Wise Lord"), the only One worthy of worship, who with his seven *Spentas* creates the material and the spiritual universe. Through his holy spirit, the *Spenta Mainyu*, he creates the world, mankind and all that is good in it; through the six other spirits, the *Amesha Spentas* ("holy immortals"), the rest of universe is created. *Ahura* is the source of "The Truth" ("*asa*"), but he is not necessarily omnipotent (all-powerful), and is referred to as "the Better."

His creation of law, order and truth is threatened by a inferior god, *Angra Mainyu*, a creature perhaps above the *Spentas*, who by free will chooses evil and therefore is responsible for "The Lie" ("*druj*"), and who seems to have creative ability as well, only he creates the negative things. The conflict between "The Truth" and "The Lie" (good and evil) is carried out not by these gods personally, but by their respective creations. Although *Ahura* will win and this dualism will apparently cease, the outcome depends heavily upon mankind who by its support speeds up the inevitable victory of the good.

Each human is given "free will" to choose which side he/she will be on, which once made cannot be reversed. The follower of "The Truth" (the

30

"*ashavan*") must avoid lies, support the poor, perform several kinds of sacrifices, and so on, thereby achieving integrity and immortality. "The Truth" is portrayed by the ordered society of the herdsmen and farmers, "The Lie" by the thieving and destructive nomads.

There will be a Last Judgment, where those who follow "The Lie" are condemned both by their conscience and then by *Ahura* to Hell and those of "The Truth" enter Heaven. The difficult part is that there is no concept of forgiveness of sins: one must hope that the abundance of one's "good deeds, good words and good thoughts" will be greater than the negative in their lives.

3. Daniel

Zoroaster and the Jews

In the early sixth century BC, Daniel is among the young Jewish nobility carried off to Babylon and trained as advisor to the Babylonian court. After the Persian conquest of Babylon, he is the first of the "three presidents" of the empire under the reign of Darius the Mede, who also names him as chief ("*Reb-Mag*" [see Jeremiah 39:3, 13]) of the hereditary caste of the Magi [Daniel 4:9; 5:11; 6].

There is confusion as to Zoroaster's dates. Linguistic analysis of the writings attributed to him suggests that he lives around 1200-1000 BC, which is only a few centuries after Israel's Exodus from Egypt. However, tradition gives the years 628-551 BC as his lifetime. He supposedly converts Hystaspes, father of Darius, to this new religion, although the name Zoroaster is not mentioned in any cuneiform writings. As to the theology, prior to this period, there are no representations of *Ahura*; however, starting with Darius there are invocations and representations of *Ahura Mazda* alone on royal inscriptions (the *Behistun Inscription* written by Darius I contains many references to *Ahura*) until Artaxerxes II, when invoking a triad: *Ahura, Mithra, Anahita*, begins.

So Zoroaster's influence is in its early stages during Daniel's stay in Babylon and Persia, which may explain some of their willingness to accept Daniel's emphasis in regard to the One God of the universe. As an aside, the Bible does demonstrate that there are others who apparently do worship the true God, besides those who are in the stream of Abraham's family. The oldest book of the Bible (based upon how ancient the Hebrew is in which it is written) is the book of Job, who is thought to be contemporary to Abraham. There is also Melchizedek, who literally appears from nowhere [Hebrews 7:1-4], and, as "a priest of God Most High" [Genesis 14:18-20], he receives the tithe from Abraham.

So indeed others may know God, but this defines the very difficulty the Jews have in Persia: on the surface the two religious systems seem very comparable, so how then does one know whether he is on the right track? As one digs deeper into such things as Covenant, atonement and forgiveness, the divergence between the Bible and Zoroaster becomes manifest. Therefore the Jewish solution is wise: by forming the synagogues and emphasizing teaching, God's Word is constantly kept before the people, equipping them with a foundation to not again become sloppy about their relationship to God (which ultimately had been the reason for which their exile began).

The Magi's Exposure to the Jews

What a challenge it must be for Daniel to be in charge of the group that is the guardian of Zoroaster's teachings. One can only imagine the discussions (or arguments?) that they have. Yet in the process Daniel identifies to at least some of the Magi the prophesies of the Jewish faith: the

Lion of Judah [Genesis 49:9; Numbers 24:9]; Balaam's prophecy of Numbers 24:17, "A Star shall come out of Jacob, a Scepter shall rise out of Israel"; Isaiah 7:14's "Behold, the young woman/virgin shall conceive and bear a Son, and shall call His Name Immanuel"; Isaiah 60:3's "The Gentiles shall walk to Your light, and kings to the brilliance of Your dawning"; and of Daniel's own prophecy[48] in chapter 9, concerning the timing of the Messiah, the Prince, Who would be "cut off" [v 26].

Perhaps they are disturbed by Proverbs 30:4's "Who has established all the ends of the earth? What is His Name, and what is *His Son*'s Name, since you know?" or the suffering servant of Isaiah 53:4-6 (and other passages):

> Surely He has borne our calamities and carried our agonies; yet we judged Him as punished, struck by God, and oppressed. But He was wounded for our rebellion, He was crushed for our iniquities; the chastisement for our peace [*SHALOM*] was upon Him, and by His stripes we are healed. All we like sheep have gone astray; each of us has turned to his own path; yet Jehovah has laid on Him the iniquity of us all.

But they never become familiar with the prophesy in regard to the birth in Bethlehem in Micah 5:2, which consequently requires the Magi to come to Herod, asking "Where is He…?"

Daniel 9's Prophecy

Mention should be made of the prophecy of the 70 "weeks" in Daniel 9:24-27.[49] Each "week" is understood to mean a "Sabbath Year" period of 7 years (the "Sabbath Year" being the last year of each set of 7). The 70 "weeks" is made up of a 7 "week" (49 year) period, plus a 62 "week" (434 year) period (total of 483 years), and a final "week" (7 years). The prophecy is comprised of the following elements:

A chronological summary of Daniel 9:24-26:
1. There would be a decree to rebuild Jerusalem.

2. Jerusalem and the Temple would be rebuilt.
3. Then an anointed one (messiah) would be "cut off" (an idiom for "rejected" or "killed").
4. Then Jerusalem and the Temple would be destroyed again.[50]

Now of course, the sticky part is which of the four edicts is the one from which to start counting this prophetic period:

1. The decree from Cyrus in 539 BC.
   (see Ezra 1:1-4; unlikely time frame)
2. The decree from Darius in 519 BC.
   (see Ezra 5:3-7; unlikely time frame)
3. The decree from Artaxerxes to Ezra in 457 BC.
   (see Ezra 7:11-16)
4. The decree from Artaxerxes to Nehemiah in 444 BC.
   (see Nehemiah 2:1-8)[51]

If a "prophetic year" of 360 days is used, times 69 years equals 173,880 "Julian Days"; using a normal 365.25 day year, the total would be 176,415 "Julian Days." Adding the prophetic year days to (*Nissan* 1, March 26? [52]), 457 BC renders April 16, 20 AD; adding a normal year days produces March 26, 27 AD. Adding the prophetic year days to (*Nissan* 1, March 5?), 444 BC yields March 26, 33 AD[53], while adding a normal year days brings March 4, 40 AD. None are near the birth of Jesus, and the closest to His death is the March 26, 33 AD date.

Verse 26 says "after" the 62 "weeks" (which follows the first 7 "weeks"; total: 69 "weeks"), the Messiah, the Prince, "will be 'cut off,' but not for Himself" – reasonably the description is of Jesus and His death, as per Isaiah 53. Possibly the 70th "week" describes His ministry ("confirm the Covenant" – perhaps including the Last Supper?) and midway through the "week" (three and a half years) may refer to the death of Jesus ("put an end to sacrifice and offering"), however the second part of the previous verse talks of the people of a prince (the Romans) who will destroy the temple and

34

the city. That event comes 37 years after Jesus' death, over 5 "weeks" after Jesus' death, so what exactly is being described is not clear.

At best, the prophecy deals with the death of Jesus. Although the Magi likely were exposed to this prophecy, would it help cause them to journey to Palestine for His birth? Would they have known that He would be about 30-33 years old for them to count backwards to His birth? Indeed, the prophecy may be useful for us, but it seems unlikely that they would have benefited from it, without something more specific added on, which has not been handed down to us.

4. Charlatans (Astrologers and Magicians)

The Study of the Stars: A Blended Science

[Jehovah,] Who speaks to the Sun and it does not rise, and for the stars He sets a seal; by Himself He stretches out the heavens, and treads on the heights of the sea; He made the Great Bear, Orion, and the Pleiades, and the chambers of the south; Who does great things beyond searching out, yes, wonders beyond number.   Job 9:7-10

Some Bible translations such as the *New English Bible* or the *Revised English Bible*, translate "Magi" simply as "astrologers." Is this a good translation? Not really, because the word as it is used today is heavily laced with images of charlatans, quackery, and mere superstition. It betrays a lack of understanding of who the Magi are and of the science of the stars throughout history.

One of the "fathers" of modern astronomy, Johannes Kepler, is especially noted as establishing rules of planetary orbits and particularly that the Sun is at one of the focal points of a planet's elliptical orbit. These rules are the foundation of today's space missions – for instance, in determining how to aim a space ship so that it will be in the place where its target planet will actually be. Yet "at least 800 horoscopes drawn up by Kepler are still extant"[54] – so, should he simply, merely be referred to as "Kepler, the astrologer," as apparently is happening in regard to the Magi? Is that term an accurate portrayal of Kepler or of the Magi or of their respective science disciplines? To do so can demonstrate ignorance of the history of the study of the stars.

As late as 1600 years after Christ (Kepler's era), the study of the stars is still a blend of astronomy and astrology (in fact, the dictionary tells us that "astrology" is the original name of the science we now call "astronomy").[55] With the earth at the center for *the reason* for the universe's existence, astrology includes the attempt to find meaning in what the universe displays – just what role do the heavens play in the affairs of the earth?

It is obvious that things happen in the sky, the realm of God's "dwelling": planets move, comets and novas suddenly appear and disappear. The Sun, Moon, and stars are created to be "for signs and seasons" [Genesis 1:14]; and in a book that is either contemporary to or predates Abraham, God claims responsibility for constellations we still recognize today: the Pleiades, Orion, the *Mazzaroth* (the Hebrew Zodiac), and the Great Bear with its cubs [Job 38:31-32; also 9:8-10 above; Amos 5:8]. "He allots the number of the stars; to them all He calls them by name" [Psalm 147:4; see Isaiah 40:26]. So, a truly godly study of the celestial part of God's creation requires what attitude from its student?

Kepler has an uneasy truce with his contemporary astrology, what he calls astronomy's "foolish daughter,"[56] cynically observing, "Nature, which has conferred upon every animal the means of subsistence, has given astrology as an adjunct and ally to astronomy"[57] – that is, astrology keeps bread on the table so that the more noble astronomy can be pursued. Rather than blindly accepting astrology's claims, he decides to check on the accuracy of his predictions, through which he concludes that the stars do not guide human life.[58] However, not *all* "astrology" is to be dismissed, to not "throw out the baby with the bathwater," because, metaphorically, "As God the Creator played music, in like manner he taught nature to play after his likeness – that is to say, precisely that music that he has played for her."[59]

Astrology's True Mission

> When I reflect on Your heavens, the work of Your fingers, the moon and the stars which You have fixed, what is man that You remember him, and the son of man that You visit him? You have made him a little lower than God, and have crowned him with glory and honor.
>
> Psalm 8:3-5

In the Bible, the word "sign" (as in "for signs and seasons" [Genesis 1:14]) usually indicates a specific type of activity of God, particularly within His Covenant relationships. Often the "signs" are two-edged, for instance, in Exodus 3:12; 4:8-9, 28-30; 7:3; 10:1-2 (and other places), they are to confirm His relationship to, and to comfort, the Covenant People of Israel. On the other hand, the *same* "signs" also are to challenge outsiders (Pharaoh and the Egyptians) that they are dealing not just with Israel but also with their Covenant-Partner, a challenge to either submit to God or to rebel and war against Him and His People ("harden the heart"). The task of the "sign" is not to draw attention to itself, but to call the human to look at God and His involvement, and therefore to look to His promises, particularly His specific revelation – His Word. The "sign" has no voice – and yet it does!

> The heavens declare the Glory of God; and the firmament proclaims the works of His Hand. Day pours forth speech to day, and night declares knowledge to night – yet there is no speech nor words, their voice is not heard; [still] their measuring line [or "musical string"] goes throughout all the earth, and their words to the end of the world. In them He has set a tent for the Sun.   Psalm 19:1-4 (see Romans 10:18)

Another key idea in the Old Testament is the word "Glory." Immediately we often think of the majesty, power, creativity of God – all the big bells and whistles. But what is fascinating is the dialog from Exodus 33:18-19:

> Moses said, "I pray, show me Your glory."
> Jehovah said, "I will make all My goodness pass before you, and will proclaim before you the [Covenant] Name 'Jehovah'; I will be gracious to whom I will be gracious, and will show mercy on whom I will show mercy...."

Apparently what God is "*most* proud of" is *not* His creativity, power, wisdom, might and control (which we immediately assume, because *we* would accent them if we were in His place), but the central message of His Glory is His goodness, mercy, grace, and Covenant. In the next chapter, when He actually does show His Glory, He adds "steadfast Love" (*Hesed*), faithfulness, forgiveness and justice. Further of interest is that these are *qualities* not objects. One cannot see a jar of grace or a box of mercy – they are observed *only in action*, therefore Moses would have to see God's Glory happen *within history* – *HIS-Story* – or "the back parts" [33:23]. Likewise it is useful to realize that Moses is not allowed to see the future, the "face" of God.

So if "the heavens are telling the *Glory* of God," should they not be directing our attention to these qualities (and therefore actions) that God Himself emphasizes? This is what astrology *ought* to do, since it desires to bring meaning to physical fact – it is the philosophical or spiritual side of astronomy.

Making Sense of "the Ballet"

The reason why this writer calls what will be following, "the Ballet" of the heavens, is due to an experience he had in his denomination's boarding high school for boys in Bronxville, NY. During this time, *the Lincoln Center for the Performing Arts* invited all the schools in the metropolitan area to send a student representative to experience the range that *the Lincoln Center* had to offer. Among the concerts and plays and the rest, there was one production that was attended about which this (teenaged) writer was *never* going to let his (male) dorm mates know – he went to a *ballet*.

The first part of the evening was probably some sort of interpretative dance that seemed like merely a lot of jumping around up on stage, and was entirely confusing to this writer. However, the second half featured a ballet based on a fairy tale. This writer knew the story! Suddenly it all made sense – this writer could *understand* what all the movement on stage was about.

Astronomy shows us what is happening on the heavenly stage, just like that ballet's first half. Astrology should be what gives us the second half, providing the basis to recognize *meaning* in regard to that activity on the stage.

Astrology and Modern Science's Failure

Astrology, as the philosophical side of astronomy, should bring us to the contemplation of God's Glory (especially as defined above), it should direct our attention to the Jehovah of Covenant – the message is about *God*, not us – which is what the Psalmist says. Kepler writes of science as "thinking God's thoughts after Him." Isaac Newton hopes that his famous *"Principia"* would "persuade thinking men to believe in a deity."

> For what can be known about God is plainly revealed to them – because God has revealed it to them! For from the creation of the world, the unseen things of God – especially His eternal power and divine nature – can be grasped and discerned by the things that are made, so they are without excuse. Although they did know God, they would not glorify Him as God nor give [Him] thanks, but they became fools in their logic, and their hearts lacking understanding were darkened. ... they changed

the truth about God into the lie and worshiped and served the creature rather than the Creator, Who is blessed to the ages! Amen.

Romans 1:19-21, 25

This discipline has become sidetracked. Jehovah is for all intents and purposes taken out of His handiwork. The "sign" has itself become the god – we are victims of the stars and planets, *they* are the ones who rule us.[60] The situation is similar to the "brass serpent," which God commands Moses to make to end the plague of serpents in Numbers 21:8-9. Originally it is a "sign" – one looks toward that which God provides according to His promise, and therefore discovers a marvelous demonstration of His Covenant and of His grace, mercy and forgiveness (His Glory). Yet centuries later, in II Kings 18:4, rather than drawing one's attention to Jehovah, *the serpent* is now worshipped as a god itself.

This is what we humans do. Astrology is the most obvious example, but it is only the forerunner of what is happening throughout the sciences. All scientific data is that first part of the Ballet, "all that jumping around up on stage." What then is the philosophical/spiritual basis by which to make sense of it, to interpret the data – what is the second half of the ballet?

We are faced with two primary approaches: "with the God of '*HIS-Story*'" or "without Him, with 'No-Story'" – that is, either *creation* or *evolution* (cosmic, biological, social and the rest). Without Jehovah, all life and all that happens is controlled by the "god" evolution, for example, there are discussions in regard to how much human behavior is "programmed" – not so much by the stars, but still by happenstance, as mere victims of a certain random DNA arrangement, one "natural" master now replacing another in control of our lives.

The difference between the Godly philosophy of a science and its alternative is that the first leads us to hope, whereas the second only brings hopelessness. When we are led to the "Glory" of God, particularly His goodness, Covenant, grace, mercy, steadfast love (*Hesed*), faithfulness, forgiveness and justice, we walk away with expectation and a(n eternal) future. Without God, we walk away as victims of uncaring, impersonal forces that control our lives and really provide nothing in regard to any real future for us and all humanity.

As one reads what one might call the "hard core evolutionists" (such as Jay Gould, Carl Sagan and others), they take evolution to its appropriate logical conclusions: evolution does not direct us to an uplifting promise, but rather to the despair that the human has no real significance, no worth and no hope. That we ever existed, evolution cares not. Is "progress" supposed to go "upward"? Evolution is not interested. There is no drive for anything, and ultimately the universe will self-destruct, either by running out of useable energy, or by retracting back into the singularity that predated the supposed "big bang." The real underlying message is that everything anyone does will eventually be negated into a nothingness; all equations end in "0" – ultimately there are no accomplishments. The logical conclusion of evolution is that "You do not matter; you do not matter at all to anything."

Most evolution-adherents are content with the immediate gratification of a God-less process which created the world (and the convenience of having no accountability to a "non-existent" Him, indeed, to not even bother with Him at all), without addressing the fact that their pet theory makes their own striving for acknowledgement a fool's errand. Everything they do is ultimately *nothing*. At the same time, the cry so often from the social sciences as to how people are lacking in self-worth and self-esteem. Programs are put into place to try to encourage people, meanwhile at the same time evolution uses its tools to utterly decimate them. Indeed how science flounders without God!

Since in regard to astrology, both the good *and* the bad philosophies are identified with only a single name, we will identify the difference by speaking of "Godly" astrology as opposed to the "corrupted" version. Our task then is to recognize God's appropriate place in His creation as it bears witness to His Glory in the heavens, properly applying Godly astrological/philosophical concepts, meanwhile attempting to avoid the abuse that "corrupted" astrology has become. This book has the same struggle that the Magi – especially as Zoroastrians – would encounter in their attempts to find meaning in the stars, so that they can be both consummate astronomers as well as Godly astrologers. Daniel, as their leader, would provide great assistance as they walk the difficult line between the two astrologies.

Magic, the Future and Other Impositions

The danger when dealing with astrology, even Godly astrology, is the tendency we humans will always have within our fallen human nature. We tend toward the mechanical when dealing with God, which is the root desire for "magic." We want orderliness and predictability. We want systematic uniformity. We laugh when a sport player refuses to wash his "lucky" article of clothing (no matter how bad it smells), lest he damage his streak of "luck." Yet how often do we feel that we have to, for instance, pray in a certain way, with certain words, with certain fervor, so that now God "really ought to listen to us"? How often have we gotten a desirable answer to prayer and then have tried to duplicate the exact same setting lest we diminish the consistency of the answer?

"Magic" at its root is that we do the same thing, in the same way, with the same "tools" in order to have the same power to get the same results *every time.* In books of magic "spells," this is taken even to the place where there are dire warnings that if *anything* is not done "properly," at best the "spell" will not work; at worst, one unleashes uncontrolled power that can put oneself in danger. Yet how often when even the Christian does not get the desired outcome of his prayer, or get the healing that he desired, or the person converted (and so forth), that he then castigates himself: perhaps he did not "believe" enough, or was not "fervent" enough, or did not do it in the right place or in the right position or for long enough, or any of the other myriad of ways in which *he "failed."*

This is really "magic" at its heart and is a big driving force behind "corrupted" astrology. It is just another way for fallen human nature to automate: to make life, the future, and even God, predictable and manageable, rather than realizing that God is a living Person, Who intimately and personally interacts with us and with this world. Not only does He respond to events around us, He declares "behold, I will do a new thing" [Isaiah 43:19] – rather than doing same thing twice, He is in the habit of doing different things – He never quite seems to fit into a box, He refuses to be subject to "magic."

This is why it is so necessary to interpret the stars by *HIS-Story* rather than to make the stars the interpreters of human affairs or the predictors of the future. For instance, there are conjunctions in the sky – some where the planet and its target are extraordinarily close – frequently. What makes *this* one the one to pay attention to? "Corrupted" astrology tells us to look to the stars themselves to "discover" the answer, usually an automated answer. Godly astrology tells us that the meaning can only be found within God's *"Story,"* only insofar as to what God has specifically revealed in His prophecies and in His acts on this earth in His sacred Word.

It is important to also realize that there is one who is eager to encourage the depersonalizing of God and the growth of the magical attitude: Satan. This is why "corrupted" astrology is so vehemently condemned in the Bible – it walks Satan's line of rebellion away from God, that of mechanizing the universe, of exalting of one's own abilities, and of trying to understand and control life and the future without needing a direct partnership with God.

"Magicians" and "Astrologers"

There is the tendency in humans to appropriate a famous person or group to help legitimize oneself. As an example, despite Kepler's dislike of astrology and rejecting the stars' influence on human life, yet because he is connected to the practice, astrologists use him to bring dignity to their occupation – therefore, the seventh version of the astrology software named "Kepler" is available (the control by the planets is supposed to be *that* mechanical!).

Zoroaster seems also be victim to the same kind of indignity. Pliny the Elder, a Roman historian, calls him the inventor of magic, yet for what writings we have that are directly connected to Zoroaster, such an pursuit seems as much out of character as the Jewish magic book, *The Seventh Book of Moses*, would be most foreign to *that* fundamental prophet of God. So therefore, although giving us a dignified word like *"magi*strate," the Magi have also become the source of the word *"magic."*

Actually, what little magical teaching that supposedly is Zoroastrian first appears only from the 14th century AD onwards. Instead, "the fabulous magus, Ostanes" supposedly is the creator of the magic arts. But even *his* "writings" are *pseudepigrapha* – writings falsely attributed to an individual.[61] We know that the magic arts are well developed by Moses' time, since he encounters magicians in Pharaoh's court, and with the Old Testament kings there are "prophets" that are not of the Lord – long before Darius, Daniel and Daniel's Magi.

One factor for the association with astrology was Zoroaster's name, or rather, what the Greeks made of it. Within the scheme of Greek thinking (which was always on the lookout for hidden significances and "real" meanings of words) his name was identified at first with star-worshiping (*astrothytes* "star sacrificer") and, with the *Zo-* [*zoe – life*], even as the *living* star. Later, an even more elaborate mytho-etymology evolved: Zoroaster died by the living (*zo-*) flux (*-ro-*) of fire from the star (*-astr-*) which he himself had invoked, and even, that the stars killed him in revenge for having been restrained by him.

The second, and "more serious" factor for the association with astrology was the notion that Zoroaster was a Babylonian. The alternate Greek name for Zoroaster was Zaratas/Zaradas/Zaratos (*cf.* Agathias 2.23-5, Clement *Stromata* I.15), which—so Cumont and Bidez—derived from a Semitic form of his name. The Pythagorean tradition considered the mathematician to have studied with Zoroaster in Babylonia (Porphyry *Life of Pythagoras* 12, Alexander Polyhistor apud Clement's *Stromata* I.15, Diodorus of Eritrea, Aristoxenus apud Hippolitus VI32.2). Lydus (*On the Months* II.4) attributes the creation of the seven-day week to "the Babylonians in the circle of Zoroaster and Hystaspes," and who did so because there were seven planets. The Suda's chapter on *astronomia* notes that the Babylonians learned their astrology from Zoroaster. Lucian of Samosata (*Mennipus* 6) decides to journey to Babylon "to ask one of the magi, Zoroaster's disciples and successors," for their opinion.[62]

So what has happened? All the sources referred to above, from Pliny the Elder to Lucian of Samosata, are all post-Bethlehem-birth authors. Truly they may have access to other material than we have, but they are also writing some 600+ years after Zoroaster, after an overlay of traditions and legends, and there is the problem of just how much *pseudepigrapha* may play into their sources.

As well, there is another problem: these authors write from a Roman Empire environment and Rome definitely does not like Persia – this is why we in the west, whose culture is based upon Rome's ideology, know so little in regard to the Persians and commonly hear so little about the Persian role in regard to Bethlehem's birth.

5. Rome *really* does not like Persia, Persia likes the Jews

Persia Subsidizes the Jewish Rebuilding

When the Jews are permitted to return to the Promised Land, Persia subsidizes the rebuilding of Jerusalem and its Temple (the books of Nehemiah and Ezra). Many Jews are in prominent positions (for example, Daniel and Esther). Although in the intervening years Alexander conquers the Middle East, and then after his death the empire is broken up, the Persians seem to maintain their interest in the Jews, as well as reviving their interest in Zoroaster's "one God."

Rome is Embarrassed

In 63 BC, Pompey conquers Jerusalem, then attacks the Persian outpost in Armenia, although Persia does not respond. However, in 55 BC, Crassus and his legions sack Jerusalem and go on to attack Persia. He is decisively defeated at Carrhae, losing 30,000 troops and his life as well, because Rome does not effectively handle Persia's *Cataphracti* – not a chariot cavalry, but a highly mobile *mounted* cavalry. In the ancient world, Persia has the finest cavalry units in the world and they *always* ride horses; camels are only used for baggage. Their response to Rome is an invasion of Armenia, Syria, and Palestine.

Roman rule in Palestine is reestablished under Antipater, Herod's father, who then has to run before yet another Persian invasion in 40 BC. Mark Antony reestablishes Roman sovereignty in 37 BC and repeats Crassius' foolishness (although he survives). Persia then sweeps Rome out of Palestine: Jewish sovereignty is restored and a Jewish garrison fortifies Jerusalem.

Herod himself flees to Rome, there to be designated "King of the Jews"; yet it is three years of war and five months of a siege of Jerusalem before he can sit on his throne.

Combine Suspicion of Science with Embarrassment

It is a curious footnote of history that although the empire is Roman, strangely, *Greek* is its common ("*Koinē*") language. That is because Latin reflects Rome's practical, efficient, and mechanical genius, but *Greek* will be essential to the spread of Christianity – it supplies the language for the "higher" pursuits, particularly of philosophy/spirituality. The Greeks are very keen on the intricacies of math and physics, and even toy with the idea of the "unseen," such as the undivided basic units ("atom-") of matter.

The Greeks, fascinated by the exotic, are intrigued by what they see in foreign Babylon and Persia: they observe "astrology" such as they did not practice, and scientific arts that they label as "magical" – not so much occult and supernatural, rather they are of the *genre* of the Magi. But in Rome's awkwardness about the sciences and their hostility toward Persia (humans often vilify their enemies), Rome dismisses the Magi as charlatans, merely "magicians" and "astrologers." It is an epithet that creeps into the book of Acts: Elymas [Acts 13: 6, 8] and Simon (Simon "*Magus*") [Acts 8: 9, 11] are *Rome*'s view of the "Magi."

Do the Magi practice the occult? We know that "magicians" with a well developed art already exist in Joseph and Moses' times, persons with such "secret" knowledge are often advisors to kings, and possibly the Persians would not be immune to this influence. Yet it is not "a given" that all or even most of the Magi would be involved in the dark arts, especially if they shared Zoroaster's rejection of the evil god, *Angra Mainyu*.[63] The evidence of Matthew's Gospel is that there are indeed those who do hold to Daniel's

God and His prophecies to the degree that they would travel into enemy territory to "come to worship Him" [Matthew 2:2].

IV. Setting Up for The Ballet

God said, "Let there be lights in the heavens ... let them be for Signs ... Genesis 1:14

A. Significant Action: Retrograde Motion

A key element in this heavenly ballet is what astronomers call "retrograde motion." This is when a planet appears to stop, reverse motion and travel backwards. Then it again stops and resumes forward motion. In reality nothing of the kind has happened – it is only a trick of perspective. Perhaps it can be understood as when we 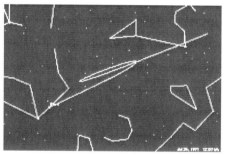 are driving down a road parallel to a train some distance to the side: is it travelling slowly, is it moving at all? Did it really pass that bush, or is it merely that since we have changed observation points, it only *appears* to have passed the bush. As it fades behind us, we cannot even be sure if it is backing up.

When the earth, in an inner and therefore faster orbit, passes by a planet in an outer orbit, as one looks against the unmoving distant backdrop of the stars, there is the same problem. As the earth approaches the outer planet, both are going forward, but as the earth catches up, the outer planet looks like it is going 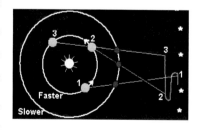 backward, until finally as the earth makes the turn to go around the Sun, now the outer planet appears to be heading forward normally.

As might be guessed, this happens frequently – every year in regard to every outer planet. But in particularly the Christmas celestial Ballet, what is seen from the earth tells a most amazing story. It is like the letters in the alphabet. By themselves there really is nothing special or unusual about them. Yet they can be put together into such a way that a really powerful message can be conveyed. Of such significance is this Ballet.

B. The Royalty of the Skies

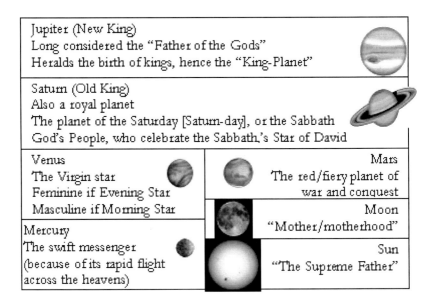

Jupiter (New King)
Long considered the "Father of the Gods"
Heralds the birth of kings, hence the "King-Planet"

Saturn (Old King)
Also a royal planet
The planet of the Saturday [Saturn-day], or the Sabbath
God's People, who celebrate the Sabbath's Star of David

Venus
The Virgin star
Feminine if Evening Star
Masculine if Morning Star

Mars
The red/fiery planet of war and conquest

Mercury
The swift messenger
(because of its rapid flight across the heavens)

Moon
"Mother/motherhood"

Sun
"The Supreme Father"

C. Conjunctions

1. Close-enough Encounters

As a planet meets a star or another planet, they do not have to touch to qualify as a conjunction – in fact, most of the time they only have to be in the same general neighborhood. In very rare cases when they do come close to touching, the result can be most impressive. And, if the planet is in

50

retrograde motion, then the conjunction occurs three times, even more emphasizing the significance of the meeting to the viewer.

7 BC - Jupiter Meets Saturn Three Times

In 1604, Johannes Kepler observes Jupiter (the "new king") passing Saturn (the "old king") in the constellation Scorpio/Ophiucus. He later determines that in 7 BC, there is a rare triple conjunction in Pisces: Jupiter passes Saturn, then *both* planets stop and reverse course; again Jupiter passes Saturn and again both stop; they start forward and for the third time Jupiter passes Saturn. One such conjunction between these two great planets is thought of as the passing of power from the old to the new ruler – but three times? With the fish being a symbol of Christianity, that this event occurs in Pisces would seem to be especially significant.

2. Massing Events

Feb 20, 6 BC – Mars and the New Moon – the Evening Stars

Not long after Jupiter and Saturn's last conjunction, Mars comes scooting from the Sun and forms a loose triangle with them. This is a "massing," that is, when three or more celestial bodies come together within a fairly "close" location. Then the new Moon, "new mother," enters the picture and actually covers Saturn and then Jupiter. It

suggests that a birth is immanent that would cause a "transfer of power" from "an old ruler" to "a new ruler," by conflict (Mars), perhaps reflecting John 12:31: "Now is the judgment of this world, now shall the ruler of this world be cast out." *And/or* it could mean that a birth is coming that brings about a transition from an old rule (the Old Covenant, with its Saturn-day

[Saturday] Sabbath) to a new rule, also through conflict (the cross). Yet as notable as all this is, Kepler does not think that this is the Star of Bethlehem, but only its prelude.

Spring 5 BC – A New Celestial Event Appears

A short time later, in that same general area, Kepler observes a new nova – this he feels is the more likely candidate for the "Star." Unknown to him, ancient Chinese records do record something: William's Comet Catalog of 1871 identifies two events – one in 5 BC and a second in 4 BC. The first is a "hut" event in Capricornus, a "sweeping star" or "broom star" with a tail or rays, visible for about 70 or more days, probably a comet. The second is a "po," or tailless event in Aquila. Unfortunately the Chinese words are not as specific as we might wish.

However now come the problems that many Bethlehem star hunters do not address: they seem to jump at *any* event in *any* place in the sky as a possible candidate. But there are some criteria that must be met: first, the occurrence must be in a place where the Magi definitely recognize it as significantly touching on the Jews in Palestine. There must be something specifically aligning the event to prophecy and/or to constellations associated with the Promised People, otherwise over hundreds of years the Magi would have to come repeatedly to Palestine looking for the King.

The second is that the event must move, as Matthew indicates. As an example, as eye-catching as they may be, novas and supernovas do not move. A comet does move, but again, what would indicate that it has anything to do with the Jews? As well, a comet usually is an omen of misfortune, often the sign of the death of a king or the fall of an empire. Not only must the event move, it also has to stop and stand "over where the young Child was."

The third is that, because Herod had children two years and under killed, the celestial event in question likely has to span over at least a year. Neither of the two Chinese candidates last more than a few months.

D. The Constellations

1. Changing "the Great Month"

There is a noteworthy side issue here: roughly around Jesus' life, "the Great Month" changes. What this refers to is that the earth's tilt makes its axis point in the general direction of one of the signs of the Zodiac. Because of the earth's spin, the axis travels in the opposite order (precesses) from the Sun's normal yearly journey through the constellations. The Zodiac is divided into 12 units, each comprising a 30° arc in the heavens (1/12 of 360°, and may or may not correspond to the actual size of the representing constellation). Since it is thought to take a "Great Year" of about 25,920 years to travel the full circuit, each "Great Month" should represent around 2,160 years. The "Age" or "Great Month" boundaries are subject to all kinds of debate, so it is difficult to nail down exactly when such a change-over occurs.

Looking at constellations that identify the ages, it is useful to remember how God challenges Job:

Can you bind the bands of the Pleiades, or loosen the cord of Orion? Can you bring out *Mazzaroth* [the Hebrew Zodiac] in its season? Or can you guide the Great Bear with its young? Do you know the customs of the heavens? Can you set their authority over the earth?   Job 38:31-33

Jehovah indicates that He is responsible for the stage for this great Ballet. The constellations we are familiar with already exist from of very old and have a surprising consistency throughout the ages, despite the fact that the figure which represents a constellation is likely not identified based on an obvious star pattern (or lack of one) within it. Even non-Biblical traditions indicate that the constellation origins go back to Adam's son Seth, or his descendent Enoch, which then also suggests that these signs are indeed linked to "HIS-Story" – here, the prophecies – in the Bible.[64]

On this basis, Virgo is illustrated as holding a sheaf of grain, that is, in picture form bears the "Seed" – which according to Genesis 3:15 will be the human "Seed" that puts an end to the Serpent (Satan). The "Decans," or minor constellations associated with the main ones, would further the image since one is that of a woman holding a child. There are three constellations having heroes, two with a wounded foot, that are crushing the heads of snakes and scorpions, which also reflect the Genesis promise.

Despite how these themes have been overlaid with traditions and myths, since God did assemble the heavens as *His* stage, and since Genesis 1 indicates that in His design the earth is cast in an important role, then these constellations as viewed from the earth do have *something* to which they witness. The attempt in this book is not to be definitive, but rather to go back to some of the most ancient of legends surrounding the constellations of interest, to recognize that even in the non-Biblical world there are concepts which reflect the great Biblical themes.

It is important to keep in mind the above discussion in regard to the Ballet and "corrupted" astrology. Without the *"HIS-Story"* in hand, "all that jumping around on stage" is subject to mere conjecture, no matter how sophisticated that speculation appears. The stars can only show a limited description of that which only God must more precisely describe. And, again, the *"HIS-Story"* is focused on God and His Covenantal Plan of the ages, not on dictating to humans on how their individual lives are governed by impersonal (even if dressed up as godly) "influences" of the stars and planets. God's personal direct involvement in human life is not by the power of the stars, but by the power of His Word and His Holy Spirit – and He *does* have *personal* involvement in our lives.

2. The Precession of the Ages

Since we are currently near the end of "the Age of Pisces, the Fish," we step back to what may be the first "Age," that is, the "Age" of creation, and then follow the earth's axis as it precesses through the Zodiac from Cancer toward Leo.

Cancer

This is a fascinating constellation – its stars are more faint than bright, there seems to be nothing to draw our attention to it. In fact, some feel that since it is a "dull" but sizeable area of the Sun's path, a constellation had to arbitrarily be given to it. Yet it is a very ancient constellation and has always been associated with water. In Egyptian astrology it is represented by two turtles known as "the Stars of the Water,"[65] and is the ruler of "the Fourth House," known as "the 'Womb of Eternity,' where all things come into being and pass out of being at the appointed time": "the House of Genesis and also of Nemesis." In its center is "the Beehive Cluster" (modern name) which has been called "the Manger" (*Praesepe*).

The turtles in the water could be a very figurative way of describing Genesis 1:6 "Let there be a firmament in the midst of the waters, and let it divide the waters from the waters," evocative of a great turtle rising to the surface and "separating" the waters (which some "creation" myths also seem to follow).[66] Perhaps "nothing" may be a good word for Cancer! Here at the beginning of the "Great Months" is something that, reflecting Genesis 1, is the constellation that speaks of creation – creation out of "nothing."

Gemini

The sign of Gemini has an interesting history. In Hindu mythology, Yama and his twin sister Yami, later his wife, are the first couple to inhabit the earth; Yama is the first man, who dies and is the lord of the underworld, while Yami is the goddess of death. It would seem to be a succinct allegory of Genesis 2 and 3, of the creation of the woman from the rib of man, of her bringing death as she eats of the forbidden fruit, and of how "in Adam, all die" [I Corinthians 15:22].

Some depictions of "the Twins", going back at least to the time of Jesus' birth, are nude male and female figures walking hand in hand, which may be why early Christians considered them to be Adam and Eve. Easily we could think of this "Great Month" as "the Age of the Fall."

There is a further twist because in Babylonian astrology, the Twins are called "The One who has arisen from the Underworld [the dead]" along with "the Mighty King." This interpretation seems to reflect how the Lord in Genesis 3, particularly in His curse of the serpent, wove the promise of a Redeemer and Life into the midst of the death brought by sin.

Taurus

Next is Taurus, the bull. The Hebrew word for "bull" comes from *parar*, which means "to break, frustrate, invalidate" in the sense of violating or reneging on truth and Covenant (in 23 out of the 53 times *parar* is used, Covenant is "broken"), which may be why the bull is a main sin offering. This is the early Hebrew Zodiac's first constellation, represented by the first letter in their alphabet, Aleph. The association of this constellation with a bull is worldwide, even tribes in South America call it "the Jaw of the Ox." The Egyptians feel that humanity was created while the Sun passed through Taurus and is a sign linked with the renewal of life in spring. Greek myth has Zeus become a bull who carries his love (Europa) across the waters to

Crete. Perhaps it signifies not the creation of mankind, but rather its "recreation," since if we follow Biblical chronology, the Age of Taurus might be marked by the judgment of Noah's Flood, which also declares the renewal of life and human life – with Noah and his family offering sacrifices upon leaving the ark and the Covenant of the Rainbow; also with the rebirth of civilization and sadly its Tower of Babel.

Aries

In the Babylonian zodiac, in the early third millennium BC, the vernal (spring) equinox is marked by the Pleiades, but by the 7th century BC (prior to Daniel) the line has migrated to Aries. Originally the sign may have been associated with Dumuzi the Shepherd, but now is seen as the Ram (Hamal or Ari) and becomes prominent as the leading sign in the Babylonian zodiac, carrying the idea of a new beginning.

In Greek mythology, the child Phrixus (and his sister Helle, who later accidentally drowns) are to be sacrificed to the gods, but the gods are induced to send a golden ram to carry the children to safety. The ram arrives at the last moment before the sacrifice. After the rescue, at the ram's request, Phrixus sacrifices it as his substitute to the god Zeus, and it is taken up to heaven (to be represented by this constellation).[67]

Roughly 2100 years (about an "age"-worth) before Christ is Abraham[68], who is the originating point for Israel, the People of the Promise; one of the key events in his life is the "almost" sacrifice of Isaac, where a ram becomes his son's substitute [Genesis 22:13]. The ram[69] is "the Trespass Offering" [Leviticus 5:15-18; 6:6]; "the ram of atonement" [Numbers 5:8]; "the ram of consecration" of the priests [Exodus 29; Leviticus 8]; "the ram of the Whole Burnt Offering" (whole dedication of oneself) [Leviticus 9:2] and "the ram of the Peace Offering" (a communion between God, the officiating priest – usually representing the whole People –, and the individual) [Leviticus 9:4,

18]. Ram skins dyed "Bloody" red make up the covering for *the Tent of Meeting* (the Israelites' wilderness temple [Exodus 26:14]), where man meets God in a "tent" covered by "Blood."

In many ancient astrologies, Aries, the Ram (and Israel's "sign"), is considered the beginning of the Zodiac, and its "Great Month"[70] is starting as Jehovah calls Abraham: indeed it is "the beginning" as God's plan of salvation now becomes irrevocably identified with a specific family, *"HIS-Story"* now begins in earnest, and "the Age" will end only when the Messiah long promised to Abraham walks the earth. Although "the Age" is past, the Ram is not finished, as Francis Rolleston reminds us: "Aries, the Lamb that had been slain, … now is overcoming as Lord of lords (Rev 17:14)."[71]

Pisces

On the other hand, "the Great Month" the world enters within Jesus' earthly existence is "the Age of Pisces," which coincides with the beginning of the *Christian* era, a startling connection, considering what "the sign of the Fish" (not the constellation) means to the followers of Jesus. In the early centuries of this Christian "Age," they use a Fish made by two intersecting arcs as a secret sign to recognize fellow Christians especially during persecution. The letters of the Greek word for fish, *ichthus,* are an anagram for "Jesus Christ, God's Son, Savior," and are therefore also a simple confession of faith. Everything that the Ram has been in Israel now is accomplished by this Fish. Additionally, Jupiter "rules" this constellation, and Jupiter in this Ballet is *"His* star" according to the Magi.

Associating this constellation with fish is very widespread and very ancient. In Islamic astronomy, this area of the sky is known as "The Large Fish." The Babylonians see it as two fish swimming in two converging streams of water mirroring the Tigris and Euphrates rivers. It is curious that most depictions are of two fish tied together: for the Christian, two natures

(God and man) are "tied" into one Person in Jesus; also two Covenants (the Old and the New) are tied together in Jesus. It is thought that the band holding these two together springs from the forefeet of Aries and some see the fish as swimming in the waters that pour from Aquarius, which is next in the Zodiac.

Aquarius

"The Great Month of Pisces" is in our time drawing toward its close and we look forward to "the Age of Aquarius, the Water-Bearer." Aside from the predictions of modern astrologers,[72] the Bible has many references to water, but especially to "*Living* Water." "The Sacrifice of the Red Heifer" [Numbers 19] involves "Living Water" as an antidote to death's contamination of the Israelite's life; Jehovah describes Himself as "the Fountain of Living Waters" [Jeremiah 2:13; 17:13] and in Zechariah [14:8] the end time will be characterized by "Living Waters shall go out from Jerusalem." In the New Covenant is the climax: "For I will pour Water on the thirsty one, … I will pour My Spirit on your descendants, and My blessing on your offspring" [Isaiah 44:3], as Jesus declares: "He who believes in Me, as the Scripture has said, out of his innermost being will flow rivers of Living Water (but this He said concerning the Spirit…)" [John 7:38-39]. One of the main characteristics of Revelation's New Jerusalem is "the pure river of the Water of Life" [22:1] – if indeed this is the keynote for the Age of Aquarius, then indeed Pisces does swim in its water. Whether this describes heaven, or "the thousand year reign of Christ" or whatever, it is up to the choice of the reader.

3. Starting from the Other Beginning

We have to stop here in searching for the great Biblical themes in the "Ages" or "Great Months." We cannot anticipate beyond Aquarius, if indeed there will be a further "Age" beyond that one. But we have traveled only through half of the Zodiac! What about the other six constellations? No, our look at the Zodiac is not finished: we now start at its opposite end, following as the Sun begins its journey in Leo, to find the themes contemporary to the life of Jesus.

Curiously, to have two beginning points is not uncharacteristic of the Bible! The other important "year" timekeeper, the Hebrew/Jewish calendar, also has two beginning points. The year's original beginning once was the New Year (*Rosh HaShanah*), but after the Exodus that festival now falls in the *seventh* month (that is, the beginning of the second half of the year). At the Exodus, Jehovah declares that *the Passover* month becomes Month 1 for the Israelites [Exodus 12:2]. In contemplating the stars' ballet for Jesus, we also make a new beginning.

Leo

The Lion has always been associated with rulership and divinity. It stands as a guardian against darkness and evil, and its symbols often are seen in palaces, temples, and in the rituals of the Chinese New Year. Leo is the King Constellation, the head of the Zodiac; and Regulus, its brightest star, is the King Star – the King of the King Constellation, the King of Kings. In Genesis 49:8-11, Judah's Offspring is the ruling Lion:

> Judah, *you* your brothers shall praise, *your* hand shall be on the neck of your enemies; *to you* the sons of your father shall bow. Judah is a lion's whelp; from the prey, my son, you have risen up. He lies down like a lion, with his legs folded under; and who would rouse one like a lioness? The scepter shall not depart from Judah, nor a governor from between his feet, until the Peaceful One comes; and to Him shall be the obedience of the people. Binding His foal to the vine, and His donkey's colt to the choice vine, He washed His garments in wine, and His clothes in the Blood of grapes.

At the other end of the Bible, in Revelation 5:5, Jesus is "the Lion of the tribe of [the Lion] Judah, the Root of David," and in 17:14 and 19:16, He is "Lord of lords and King of kings," "with a robe dipped in Blood" [19:13].

Virgo

The Virgin is, well, a virgin. She is one of only three constellations depicting women: Virgo is the maiden, Andromeda is the mother, and Cassiopeia is the "senior." As the virgin goddess Iustitia ("Justice") or Astraea, Virgo holds the scales of justice (Libra) in her hand. As mentioned above, she also is associated with "the Seed": in Babylon, this constellation is known as "The Furrow" – the ground ready to receive "the Seed" that means life to the people; she also is represented by a sheaf of grain or corn ("the Seed"), and is often pictured as holding a palm frond in the other hand.

Libra

This is the only Zodiac sign that does not represent something living, and its origins go back to the beginning of astrology. In Babylon, it is the tool of the Sun God Shamash, guardian of truth and justice: Zabanitu judges – "weighs" – the souls of the dead to determine their destiny. In Egypt, Anubis uses a feather on one side as the counterbalance to judge the heaviness of the human heart. Frances Rolleston adds:

> In the Persian sphere, the First Decan was a man as in wrath, holding a balance in one hand, a lamb in the other. [Its Hebrew name,] Thau, bound or limit, *finished*, is the name of the last letter of the Hebrew alphabet, originally in the form of a cross. Long before the Christian era, the cross was a most sacred emblem among the Egyptians. A few days before the sun entered Aries, the ancient Persians had the feast of the cross.[73]

Scorpio

Scorpio is curious – it has four different depictions: the scorpion, the eagle, the phoenix and the serpent. In the Babylon Zodiac it is "the [creature with] a burning sting," which suggests Paul's quote of Hosea 13:14 (*Septuagint* translation): "'O death, where is thy sting? O grave, where is thy victory?' The sting of death is sin; and the strength of sin is the law" [I Corinthians 15:55-56]. There are attempts to relate this sign with the "eagle" faces in the visions of Ezekiel 1:4-10, 15-21 and Revelation 4:6-8.

Prominent within this constellation is the decan of Ophiucus, who in the Babylonian Zodiac represents *Nirah*, a serpent-god sometimes depicted with his upper half human but serpents for legs. But in the 4th century BC, Ophiucus is a man who *wrestles* with a serpent:

> The earliest mention of the constellation is in Aratus, informed by the lost catalogue of Eudoxus of Cnidus (4th century BC) [Henry George Liddell, Robert Scott, *A Greek-English Lexicon*]:
> … the starlit Ophiuchus himself: so brightly set beneath his head appear his gleaming shoulders. They would be clear to mark even at the midmonth moon, but his hands are not at all so bright; … Yet they too can be seen, for they are not feeble. Both firmly clutch the Serpent, which encircles the waist of Ophiuchus, but he, steadfast with both his feet well set, tramples a huge monster, even the Scorpion, standing upright on his eye and breast. Now the Serpent is wreathed about his two hands – a little above his right hand, but in many folds high above his left. [trans. Mair, A. W. & G. R. Loeb Classical Library Volume 129. London: William Heinemann, 1921][74]

and Rolleston's description:

> There is then the figure of a man grasping a serpent as in conflict, his foot on the head of a scorpion, whose reverted sting appears to have wounded his heel.[75]

The change in depicting Ophiucus (as well as other constellations) poses a thought: could the concept of Ophiucus have been "corrected" in the

Babylonian Zodiac from its "corrupted" original because of Daniel's influence, bringing it back to its true message? This is, of course, conjecture and cannot be tested.

Sagittarius

Greek mythology speaks of Centaurs who combine the primitive, untamed animal (horse) with ancient cultured wisdom (man). Their best representative is Chiron, whom the gods take and educate. In response, he tutors the great heroes of ancient Greece. When he is wounded, he is in such great pain that he gives up his immortality and dies. The Sumerians describe this constellation by two words, *Pabil*, meaning "elder paternal kinsman" and *Sag*, meaning "chief, head," to form the name *Pabilsag*, "the Forefather" or "the Chief Ancestor." The Babylonians depict him with wings, two heads (one panther and one human), firing an arrow aimed at the star Antares, "the heart of the scorpion."

One indeed might think of the literary type called "the Christ-figure" in terms of Chiron, with his two natures, his mission to disciple, and his giving up immortality to die. One might think of a depiction (corrupted) of the two natures of Jesus, or even see St Paul's contrast to the two "heads" of humanity, Adam ("the chief ancestor" who brings death) and Jesus ("the Chief Ancestor" Who brings Life) [I Corinthians 15:20-22, 45]. The arrow aimed at the heart of Scorpio (with its "sting") may also suggest Jesus' defeat of Satan's power. However, as always caution must be exercised: Chiron cannot adequately describe Jesus, since Jesus is more than just a heroic great Teacher, but also is the unique Savior of the world.

Capricorn

The Sumerian god *Enki*'s symbols include a goat and a fish, which are later combined into one. Babylon also considers Capricorn as a sea-goat, its two horns representing Nineveh on the Tigris and Babylon on the Euphrates, both subjected to one sovereignty[76]; the god *Ea*, "Antelope of the Seas," wearing a cloak designed as a fish's skin, complete with head and tail, rises from the oceans to teach wisdom to land-dwelling man.

One may see Christ-like symbolism in the fish (as shown in Pisces, also two-in-one), and in the goat. For Israel, the goat is also a sin offering [Leviticus 9:15; 10:16], however, in Leviticus 16, on *Yom Kippur*, it plays a very special role: two goats comprise one sacrifice. One is killed and its Blood used to cleanse and rededicate the place of worship; the other provides a visual demonstration of forgiveness (as will be identified when *Yom Kippur* is described in further detail below). Rolleston adds this:

> Then Capricornus, the goat, the victim or sacrifice sinking down as wounded, showing that the promised Deliverer must be slain as a sacrifice.[77]

4. The Message of the Zodiac

There seems to be a parallel here to the medieval Christian churches in Europe. Since most people are illiterate when the churches are built (or at least, when construction begins), each church building becomes a sort of "poor man's Bible" incorporating *"HIS-Story"* into the architecture and the artwork. So a stained glass window of the Good Samaritan or of Mary Magdalene is not simply a picture; rather, once the person is familiar with *the Story*, then by symbolisms throughout the window the observer can recall that story and its message.

It seems that a similar idea is in mind when the Architect designs the Zodiac (*Mazzaroth*) at creation: that once *the "HIS-Story"* behind the Ballet is known, then symbolisms are sprinkled all through the sky – already identified by, perhaps, Adam and his descendents[78] – to help us recall *the*

Story and its message. But just like the artwork in the churches, *the Story* must be the guiding principle, its relationship to the "artwork" has to be clearly identified from the Bible, and only now the work of art becomes useful in the way it is intended.

It is true that one can simply dismiss this as all merely fable, but remember how an enemy actively seeking to murder Jesus is used to correctly identify the reason for Jesus' death [John 11:49-53]; and even how God uses a jackass to speak to a prophet [Numbers 22:28-30]. Is it that great a flight of fancy to think that the Creator could not build into His creation arrows that point to the greatest occasion that the Universe would ever see?

V. The Ballet of the Sky, Part 1

A. *Oh, That You Would Rend the Heavens! That You Would Come Down! ...*

When You did awesome things for which we did not look, You came down, the mountains shook at Your presence.

Isaiah 64:1-3

1. I am the root and the offspring of David, the bright morning Star.

Revelation 22:16

August, 3 BC

About mid-July, 3 BC, the Sun ("Supreme Father") enters the constellation of Leo. Around July 25, Jupiter appears *en te anatole* ("in its rising" – the special astronomical significance of a star appearing in the rays of the rising Sun). On August 9, the Sun is still between the feet of the Lion, when the almost new Moon has a close brush with Venus (below the horizon) and then, just as the Sun is rising, brushes Jupiter above the horizon, in daylight it fully eclipses Regulus, and two days later it is only a bit off from eclipsing the Sun.

August 12, 3 BC – Venus joins Jupiter

On August 12, rising at about 4:30 AM, Jupiter ("the Greater Good Fortune") and the "masculine" (morning star) Venus ("the Lesser Good Fortune") are but *four* arc minutes apart – a *very* close conjunction. Being in Leo, this is an event that might make the Magi interested.

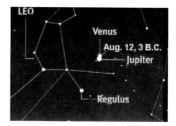

Although Jupiter is "His star," representing Jesus, so also does the masculine Venus represent Him. From the vantage point of the Ballet, this conjunction suggests the combining of the two natures, Jupiter (the New King) being the God-nature, the eternal King from the throne of God, while Venus here would be His human nature.

This is the first day of *Elul*, the month whose theme reflects John the Baptist's cry, "Repent, for the Kingdom of Heaven is at hand! ... 'Prepare the way of the LORD; make His paths straight'" [Matthew 3:2-3].

In the Jewish tradition, the month of Elul is a time of repentance in preparation for the High Holy Days of Rosh Hashanah and Yom Kippur. The word "Elul" is similar to the root of the verb "search" in Aramaic. The Talmud writes that the Hebrew word "Elul" can be expanded as an acronym for "Ani L'dodi V'dodi Li" - "I am my beloved's and my beloved is mine" (Song of Solomon 6:3). Elul is seen as a time to search one's heart and draw close to God in preparation for the coming Day of Judgment, Rosh Hashanah, and Day of Atonement, Yom Kippur.

During the month of Elul, there are a number of special rituals leading up to the High Holy Days. It is customary to blow the shofar every morning (except on Shabbat) from Rosh Hodesh Elul (the first day of the month) until the day before Rosh Hashanah. The blasts are meant to awaken one's spirit and inspire him to begin the soul searching which will prepare him for the High Holy Days. As part of this preparation, Elul is the time to begin the sometimes-difficult process of granting and asking for forgiveness. It is also customary to recite Psalm 27 every day from Rosh Hodesh Elul through Hoshanah Rabbah on Sukkoth (in Tishrei).[79]

Five days later, the still masculine Venus comes within 30 arc minutes of Regulus, although this occurs during the daytime.

Entering Virgo

On August 22, the Sun (Supreme Father) enters Virgo (Virgin). After literally chasing Venus for five days, on September 1, just after

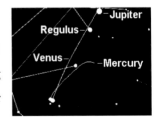

midnight, Mercury is 21 arc minutes from Venus. Speeding on ahead, Mercury enters Virgo on September 4, the next day the masculine Venus enters; meanwhile, in the following morning, the almost new Moon fully eclipses Jupiter (below horizon) and then fully eclipses Regulus (above horizon).

2. Crown the King

Jupiter meets Regulus – 1ˢᵗ Encounter – September 14, 3 BC

Jupiter approaches Regulus and through retrograde motion "crowns the King" – circles the star in a triple conjunction. On September 14, they are 20 arc minutes apart, and are in the middle of some very important celebrations and events.[80]

Rosh HaShanah

September 10 is *Tishri* 1, *Rosh HaShanah* (*The Head of the Year*), the Jewish "New Year" 3759[81] (despite *Tishri* being the *seventh* month, since *Nissan*, the month of *the Passover*, is designated the first month in Exodus 12:2). Yet *Rosh HaShanah* is important because it is considered the "birthday" of creation as well as the "anniversary" of the world's renewal, the day that "Noah removed the covering of the ark and looked, and indeed the surface of the ground was dry" [Genesis 8:13]. Observed for two days ("the long day"),[82] it has many other traditions:

This begins *Yamim Nora'im* (*The Days of Awe*) or *Aseret Yamei T'shuvah* (*The Ten Days of Repentance*), and the first *Sabbath* which falls during this period (which in 3 BC is the 14th!) is *Shabbat Shuvah* (*The Sabbath of Return*), recalling Hosea 14:1's cry, "*Shuvah Yisrael* – Return, O Israel, to the Lord your God," as also Joel 2 calls out to "Blow the trumpet in Zion, sanctify a fast, call a solemn assembly" [v 15]; and when God Himself "will turn again,

He will have compassion upon us" [Micah 7:18-20]. On *Rosh HaShanah*, God supposedly opens the heavenly books and judges the people according to their works, writing who will die and what kind of life the living will enjoy during the coming year. These ten days have the serious task of *teshuvah* – examining one's life and repenting for all wrongs committed during the previous year – perhaps God will change His judgments (this recalls Revelation 20:12: "the books were opened, and another book was opened, the Book of Life; the dead were judged out of what was written in the books, according to their works"). On *Yom Kippur* these fates will be fixed or "sealed."

This is one of the three trumpet days in the year: "*The First Trump*" is associated with Pentecost, "*The Last Trump*" is associated with *Rosh HaShanah* and "*The Great Trump*" is associated with *Yom Kippur*.[83] The *shofar*, a ram's horn, is blown one hundred times during each day of *Rosh HaShanah*, reminding people of the importance of reflection during this time [Num.29:1].[84]

It is also *Yom HaDin* (*The Day of the Trumpets*): when, heralded with trumpets, "the King is crowned" (an intriguing thought as Jupiter begins to "crown" Regulus) and begins his reign; so, as the "pre-anniversary" of Judgment Day, the trumpets celebrate God as He assumes full kingship over the earth and brings judgment against evil and the enemies of His People [Zechariah 9:14-15] – therefore it is *Yom Teruah* (*The Day of the Awakening Blast* or *The Day of the Awakening Shout*):[85]

Note that Rosh Hashanah is also called "Yom ha-Zikaron," the "Day of Remembrance" (Lev. 23:24) in reference to the commandment to remember to blow the shofar (teruah) to coronate God as King of the Universe. The blast of the shofar is meant to jolt us from our sleep. We are to remember who we really are by remembering that the LORD is our King.   John J. Parsons[86]

A famous prayer is *Avienu Malkeinu*: "Our Father, our King, answer us since though we have no deed to plead our cause, save us with mercy and loving-kindness." In Revelation 11:15, when the seventh angel blows his trumpet, the response is, "The kingdoms of this world have become the kingdoms of our Lord and of His Christ, and He shall reign forever and ever!"

This *Day of the Awakening Shout* is also when the gates of heaven are "opened," a sort of "All Saints' Day" in which those who have passed on are remembered with a resurrection emphasis, the fulfillment being the actual reuniting on the day of *THE Last Trump*, an image which Paul evokes in his letters:

> Behold, I tell you a mystery: indeed not all of us will sleep, but we all will be transformed – in a moment, in the glance of an eye, at *The Last Trumpet*. For a trumpet will sound, and the dead will be raised imperishable, and we shall be changed.　　　　I Corinthians 15:51-52

> For the Lord Himself – in a shout, in the sound of the archangel, and in a trumpet of God – will descend from heaven. The dead in Christ will rise first, then we who are alive and are left, together with them, will be taken up in clouds to meet the Lord in the air.
> 　　　　　　　　　　　　　　　　　　I Thessalonians 4:16-17

A Woman Clothed with the Sun

> Now a great sign was seen in heaven: a woman clothed with the Sun, with the Moon under her feet, and on her head a crown of twelve stars.[87] [And/Then] being with child, she cried out being in labor and in pain to give birth. Another sign was seen in heaven: behold, a great, fiery dragon having seven heads and ten horns, and on his heads seven diadems. His tail drew a third of the stars of heaven and threw them to the earth. The dragon stood before the woman who was about to give birth, that as she gives birth he will devour her Child. She bore a male Child Who was to shepherd all nations with an iron staff. And her Child was snatched up to God and His throne.　　　Revelation 12:1-5

On the second day of *Rosh HaShanah*, September 11, just after sunset, the Sun is in mid-Virgo ("clothed with the Sun"), and for two visible hours that evening, the new Moon (New Mother) is at her feet. Possibly this is the day when Jesus is born, but not necessarily so. In five verses the whole of Jesus' life is compressed, even to His ascension in the last verse. The "and/then" at the beginning of verse two could indicate a sequential event rather than a current state of being. If so, then possibly September 11 is accenting the Virgin that *conceives* and now becomes pregnant. As we will see, the idea of the *conception* is acknowledged in the Ballet, as well it should, because although at His birth God-come-into-the-flesh is revealed to the world, the real miracle occurs in the conception, where He actually takes on human flesh.

As noted above, Mercury the Messenger and the morning star (masculine) Venus are newly into Virgo. Although Venus here can represent the whole Jesus (God and Man), still its stronger emphasis is on the human nature (in contrast to Jupiter's divinity-emphasis), which again may indicate that this "sign" speaks of the conception into humanity, not the birth.

The fiery dragon presents a problem: at Virgo's feet is "the Serpent's Head" from the Serpent which Ophiucus wrestles (see above under *Scorpio*). Since both the Serpent and the Dragon represent Satan (although there is a Draco up by Polaris [the North Pole star]), one might simply assume that Revelation's Dragon would be Ophiucus' Serpent., whose head could be positioned to "catch" the newly born child. Yet why is it "fiery" since there doesn't seem to be any red stars, much less prominent ones, in the area? Did this area produce some sort of fiery comet or asteroid which breaks up into seven pieces in the atmosphere and the shower of debris might seem like the stars are falling? No record of such a thing happening has so far been found. At best, it seems that this Revelation passage indicates that the constellations are merely a "still-life snapshot" from a greater drama played out in the spiritual world – again, a sort of "poor man's Bible."

Yom Kippur

> It shall be for you an everlasting statute, in the seventh month, on the tenth of the month you shall humble your souls [fast] and do no work ... for on this day He shall make atonement for you to cleanse you; from all your sins you shall be clean before Jehovah. It is a Sabbath of Sabbath to you and you shall humble your souls [fast]. ... The priest whom He shall anoint... shall make atonement for the Holy Sanctuary, ... for the Tent of Meeting, ... for the altar he shall make atonement; for the priests, and for all the people of the congregation he shall make atonement.
> Leviticus 16:29-34

The tenth day of *Tishri*, September 19, *Yom Kippur* (*The Day of Atonement*), is regarded as the holiest day in the calendar and concludes *The Days of Awe* or *The Ten Days of Repentance*. There is fasting, attending prayer services, abstaining from forms of pleasure (such as wearing leather, washing, and wearing perfumes), making amends with each other and other rituals that, it is hoped, will achieve absolution for the Jew from the past year's wrongs. It is hoped that when the books of life and death are now sealed for the year, all will be well.

Something essential, though, is missing in the traditions just mentioned: Earlier there had been a discussion in regard to the concept of "sign" in relation to Covenant and how the stars, Sun, Moon and the planets are meant to be for "signs." As one considers, for example, the *Sabbath*, Jehovah says that it also is "a SIGN between Me and you ... that *I, Jehovah, sanctify you*" [Exodus 31:13; also Ezekiel 20:12, 20]. The *Sabbath* is *God's* evidence of Covenant, a SIGN of *His* Salvation [Deuteronomy 5:15], by which He brings His People rest (*Sabbath*) from their slavery in Egypt (when they are in their most helpless state).

The Day of Atonement is a "*Sabbath* of *Sabbath*," that is, everything that the *Sabbath* is, this day is even more so. Many activities normally allowed are not allowed here, not even to eat (that is, the people are to fast). During the Wilderness Journey, as the High Priest performs his duties, all that the people can do is merely watch – nobody else is to even be in *the Tabernacle* (*the Tent of Meeting*) during this activity. But the point is not just that they are to do nothing, rather what needs to be done must be done by another, by the anointed priest, him who "shall make atonement for you, to cleanse you" [Leviticus 16:30].

This occasion has a most interesting, picturesque, and comforting ritual of atonement, where the second goat, the scapegoat *Azazel* ("Very Removed"), after the High Priest confesses Israel's sins on it, is driven into the wilderness [Leviticus 16:8, 20-22]. What a visual reality it is, as it provides the backdrop for the Psalmist's "as far as the east is from the west, so far has *He removed* our transgressions from us" [Psalm 103:12]![88] This action is what God *chooses* to do, not because mankind has somehow persuaded Him to be merciful but because this is *His heart's* earnest desire.

Therefore this is not a self-cleaning job. The festival is not based on what one does in order to make himself right with God, but rather it is a day in which he is made right because of God's action. It is a day that is to describe God's mercy, grace and Covenant – His Glory.

This is also the day of *The Great Trump* (one of the three "trumpet" days). In researching this, most commentators are quick to jump to the "end times" and relate this to the coming of Jesus in Glory:

> Then will appear the sign of the Son of Man in heaven, and then all the tribes of the earth will wail, and they will see the Son of Man coming on the clouds of heaven with power and great glory. He will send His angels with a great trumpet sound, and they will gather His elect out

from the four winds, from one end of heaven to the other.

Matthew 24:30-31 [See also Isaiah 27:13]

But among the resources this writer surveyed, there is silence as to how this name became connected to *Yom Kippur* in the first place. So permit a conjecture: when the High Priest performs his duties (in *the Tent of Meeting* or later in *the Temple*) on this day, no one else is allowed in *the Tent of Meeting* or in *the Temple*, so if there is a problem, if he is injured or drops dead (from Divine judgment), there is no one to rescue him. Therefore a rope is tied to his foot, so that he can at least be "retrieved." Imagine the tension for all Israel – their atonement rests entirely upon the shoulders of one man, and he must get it right (acceptable) if they are to have forgiveness. Apparently the hem of his robe has little bells, which would be intensely listened for – because if they stop then the High Priest has failed to accomplish the ransom (which is what "atonement" means). There is no alternative provided in such an event. His failure would be catastrophic.

However as the sacrifices of this day are successful, likely there would be that same feeling as *our* sense of relief that comes as we hear from the lips of the acceptable Sacrifice, Jesus, "It is finished!" What more appropriate way to announce such good news than by *"The Great Trump"*! Indeed, it is an occasion for having "a big blast," and at the Last Day, when "It is finished!" comes to its full effect, indeed how appropriate that it be ushered in by the greatest of trumpet sounds.

This may also explain why *the Jubilee Year* starts on *Yom Kippur* [Leviticus 25:9]. *The Year of Jubilee* is designed by Jehovah as a time of dependence on Him – upon His goodness, grace, mercy and Covenant, that is, His Glory. For every *Sabbath* (seventh) *Year*, the land is to lie fallow, and humans and animals alike are all to share in what God has provided to be stored up in the years previous and what He gives of its own growth during this year. But then every 50th year is *the Jubilee Year*, which follows *a Sabbath Year*, and for a second year in a row the land is fallow, and one's faith is even more taxed, as one must depend on Jehovah to sustain life throughout this year as well – just as one must depend on God for atonement, so also He must be depended upon for life itself.

The Jubilee is also a restoration – a redemption (that is, an "atonement") –, where, for instance, the land reverts back to the ownership the way it is designed from the beginning, when Israel first settles the Land of Promise. So also, all Israelite slaves are restored back to their land and homes and literally everyone is given a fresh new start. One might say that this year is meant to be the "object lesson" of what *the Day of Atonement* – and the Glory of God – is about.

Sukkoth/Asif (Tishri 15-22 – September 24-October 1)

… On the fifteenth day of this seventh month shall be the Feast of Booths [Sukkoth] for seven days to Jehovah. On the first day there shall be a holy gathering. You shall do no laboring work on it …

Also on the fifteenth day of the seventh month, when you have gathered in the produce of the Land, you shall keep the feast of Jehovah for seven days; on the first day there shall be a Sabbath, and on the eighth day [day seven[89]] a Sabbath. You shall take for yourselves on the first day the fruit of beautiful trees, palm branches, the boughs of leafy trees, and willows of the brook; and you shall rejoice before Jehovah your God for seven days…

You shall live in booths for seven days. All native born in Israel shall dwell in booths, that your generations may know that I caused the children of Israel dwell in booths when I brought them out of the land of Egypt: I am Jehovah your God.   Leviticus 23:34-35, 39-43

During the five days following *Yom Kippur*, each Jewish family constructs a *sukkah*, "booth or tent," a hut made particularly from tree branches and other flimsy material, as a reminder of the frail dwellings of the Israelites in the wilderness after their Exodus from Egypt.[90] Actually, the festival is twofold: not only is this *Khag HaSukkot (the Festival of the Booths)*, but also it is *Khag HaAsif (the Festival of the Ingathering)*, the fruit harvest celebration. On the one hand, the family experiences the "roughing it" of camping, since they eat and sleep in this hut for the week, but on the other hand it celebrates the bounty that the Lord has provided now in their "settled" life.

It is simply called *"the Feast"* [I Kings 8:2, 8:65; 12:32; II Chronicles 5:3; 7:8] or *"the Feast of the Lord"* [Leviticus 23:39; Judges 21:19]; every seventh year Israel is to gather for the reading of the *Torah* during *Sukkot* [Deuteronomy 31:10-11]; King Solomon dedicates *the Temple* on *Sukkot* [1 Kings 8; 2 Chronicles 7]; and *Sukkot* is the first feast celebrated in Jerusalem after the return from captivity [Ezra 3:2-4]. But there is also a Messianic link: In Zechariah 14:16, all nations "shall go up from year to year to worship the King, Jehovah of hosts, and to keep *the Feast of Tabernacles.*" John uses the "tent" imagery to describe Jesus: John 1:14, "the Word became flesh and 'tented/camped' among us, and we beheld His Glory"; Revelation 7:15 "Therefore they are before the throne of God... and He who sits on the throne will 'tent/camp' among them"; also 21:3, "Behold, the 'tent' of God is with men, and He will 'tent/camp' with them, and they shall be His People."

In Genesis 33:17, "Jacob journeyed to Succoth, built himself a house, and made *booths* for his livestock. Therefore the name of the place is called Succoth" – a *stable* is a *"sukkah"* as well, so Jesus is born in a *sukkah!* Traditionally, for the seven days of this festival an "exalted guest" is welcomed into the family's *sukkah* – one of each of the seven *shepherds* of Israel per day: Abraham, Isaac, Jacob, Moses, Aaron, Joseph and David.

As Jesus "tents" with humanity, there is an intriguing thought: often we think "it will be heaven when we can be with God"; but according to Christmas, *Immanuel* ("God is with us"), and John[91], *for God*, heaven will be *when He gets to be with us* – basically, God anticipates when *He* can "tent" with us again.

Elsewhere in the Universe

In the meantime, throughout all these and the following conjunctions in the Ballet's first part, Saturn has begun its second leg of a retrograde motion and will spend all its time in Taurus ("the Age of Noah"?). The significance might be that the Old King, the Creator, is in the constellation that speaks of both judgment and restoration, as the better and more lasting solution to the world's evil, Jesus, is being born.

Jupiter meets Regulus – 2nd Encounter – February 17, 2 BC

Purim (Esther)

At about 3 AM, as Jupiter draws to its second Regulus encounter at about 51 arc minutes separation, the almost full Moon begins its total cover of Regulus until they all descend below the western horizon as daylight takes over. That evening, as they reappear, the Moon has moved on and *The Feast of Purim* (*Adar* 14) begins.

This celebration comes from the story of Esther, and although not a God-commanded festival, it commemorates a wonderful salvation. King Ahasuerus has taken Esther for his queen, and she keeps secret that she is a Jewess. Meanwhile, Haman, elevated to principle advisor of the king, is angry that Mordecai (Esther's uncle) will not bow to him. Rather than lay his hands on Mordecai alone, he resolves to do away with *all* the Jews in the empire. Because of Esther's courage, she exposes Haman's plan to the king just before the genocide is to begin. The "tree"/gallows that Haman has built upon which to hang Mordecai becomes the instrument of his own execution.

This feast celebrates that "he who has designed the destruction of God's People, at the seeming moment of his triumph, is himself destroyed." This is the picture of what happens on the cross, but before we get to it, permit a diversion to Genesis 3:14, "So Jehovah God said to the serpent: '... On your belly you shall go, and you shall eat dust all the days of your life.'" The snake has a curious ability: it is the only animal that can unhinge its jaw so that it can swallow something literally too big for its mouth. Imagine a snake unhinging its jaw, opening wide to swallow a huge prize, only to close on a mouthful of tasteless, useless dust.

On the cross, Satan, who has long wanted God's job, therefore has long wanted God to be out of his way, appears to be getting his heart's wish: he is putting God (the Son) to death on the cross. His hatred of God's People would be complete as he removes all hope and life from them. At the moment of Jesus' death, when Satan's mouth is opened wide in apparent triumph, he closes on a mouthful of dust and is himself defeated: "he who has designed the destruction of God's People, at the seeming moment of his triumph, is himself destroyed."

The Feast of Purim has a powerful message in regard to what the coming Jesus is to accomplish, especially in regard to Satan and his power.

Elsewhere in the Universe

Mars is in Aries, perhaps heralding the coming conflict in which the Lamb will conquer. In Pisces: the Sun highlights the Fish that is our Savior and Mercury has the Good News of victory to proclaim to the world; Venus is now an evening star (feminine), perhaps accenting how through Esther, salvation is brought to God's People, and how through Mary bearing Jesus [the Fish], salvation is brought to humanity throughout all ages.

Jupiter meets Regulus – 3ʳᵈ Encounter – May 9, 2 BC

Shavuot (Pentecost)

On May 9 (*Sivan* 6-7), two hours prior to midnight as Jupiter and Regulus (at 42 arc minutes separation) disappear behind the horizon, again the Moon, a crescent this time, touches but does not fully cover Regulus – "the King of Kings" is no longer hidden. *Sivan* 6 (and 7 for those outside of Palestine) is *Shavuot*.

The second day of *Passover* begins the seven-week "*Counting of the Omer*,"[92] after which comes *Khag HaShavuot* (*The Festival of Weeks*, Exodus 34:22, Deuteronomy 16:10) or *Pentecost* (the "Fiftieth" Day). There are two emphases in this celebration: fifty days after their Exodus from Egypt, Israel stands at the base of Mount Sinai, there to receive the *Torah*; and, as the season of the grain harvest concludes, it is also *Khag HaKatsir* (*the Festival of Reaping*, Exodus 23:16), and *Yom HaBikkurim* (*The Day of the First Fruits*, Numbers 28:26).

Remembering Israel's Sinai stop, this is *The First Trump* (all three have now sounded for Jesus' earthly arrival):

> It was on the third day, in the morning, that there were voices and lightnings, and a thick cloud on the mountain; and the voice of the *Shofar* (ram's horn) was very loud, so that all the people who were in the camp trembled... When the voice of the *Shofar* sounded long and *became louder and louder* [rather than running out of breath!], Moses spoke, and God answered him by voice.   Exodus 19:16, 19

What is this *Torah* that Israel receives at their first stop in the wilderness? "*Torah*" is often translated simply as "the Law," but it actually means

"Teachings" or "Instructions" or "Doctrines," and ultimately comprises the Books of Moses, the first five books of the Bible, "the Pentateuch." Yes, Moses receives the *Torah* on Sinai's mountaintop, and there are indeed laws, such as the Ten Commandments; but it could not be all five books, since the last three books of Moses have not yet been lived. So just what does Moses receive on the mountain?

It is important to remember our previous discussion on the Exodus 33 and 34 definition[93] of Jehovah's Glory as His goodness, Covenant relationship, mercy, grace, steadfast Love (*Hesed*), faithfulness, forgiveness and justice. Since these qualities can only be seen in action and since Moses is allowed to only see "the hinder parts," the *history* ("*HIS-Story*") in which these qualities have already been *demonstrated*, what is the history to this point? It is the book of Genesis and of *the Passover*/Exodus event itself.

Genesis reminds the Israelites about the key Covenant which has always formed the basis for their identity: Circumcision. Both Jesus and Paul declare that this extraordinary relationship comes long before the Law [John 7:22; Galatians 3:17]; it is no contract or treaty, but rather an astounding bond founded upon love and grace – God's Glory – (even an eight-day-old child and a slave, both who have no ability to commit themselves, are entered into this relationship not by invitation, but by God's *command* [Genesis 17:12-14]).[94] Since much of the rest of the *Torah* is yet to be developed throughout the rest of the wilderness journey, Genesis forms a significant foundation upon which the Sinai Covenant relationship is built, especially now in their new unity as a nation.

> The giving of the Torah was a far-reaching spiritual event—one that touched the essence of the Jewish soul for all times. Our Sages have compared it to a wedding between G-d and the Jewish people. Shavuot also means "oaths," and on this day G-d swore eternal devotion to us, and we in turn pledged everlasting loyalty to Him.[95]

The earlier festival, *Sukkoth* (*the Feast of Tabernacles*), concluded the fruit harvest; *Shavuot* now concludes the season of the grain harvest, which had started with the barley harvest before *Passover* and now seven weeks after that festival ends with the wheat harvest. The *Bikkurim* (first fruits) are brought to the Temple, which consists of "the Seven Species" of the Promised Land: wheat, barley, grapes, figs, pomegranates, olives, and dates [Deuteronomy 8:8]. At the beginning of harvest, the farmers tied a reed around the first ripening fruits from each of these species, and then now, what is identified by the reed is cut and brought in procession to the Temple. The farmers repeat Deuteronomy 26:1-10, recounting how Jacob was a homeless wanderer, how the People went into exile in Egypt, and how God redeemed them and brought them to this good Land of Promise.

Shavuot is the reminder of the precious relationship with Jehovah that His People have through Covenant, and celebrates His bounty in the harvest that is at hand. It is the initial day of the *nation* of Israel as God's redeemed People, and it is also now the initial day of *Christians* as God's also redeemed People.

Elsewhere in the Universe

This time the evening star (feminine) Venus and Mars are in Gemini, "the Age of the Fall." Mary, as she bears Jesus, fulfills the promise that the Seed of the woman will war against the Serpent [Genesis 3:15]. Martin Luther points out that already in that third chapter of the Bible, the promise speaks of a virgin birth, because everywhere else in the Bible, a child is considered the seed of the man, but *this Child* will be the seed of *the woman*.

Taurus, the sacrificial bull and "the Age of Judgment and Restoration," is highlighted by the Sun and Saturn; while Mercury bears the Good News of God's new redemption and restoration to the world.

3. A New Order Begins

June 17, 2 BC, Venus and Jupiter

Having traveled the circuit of the
Zodiac, the Sun approaches Leo again,
meanwhile Jupiter has now taken its leave
from Regulus and sets its sights toward
Virgo. The feminine Evening Star Venus
joins Jupiter on June 17, 2 BC, at an

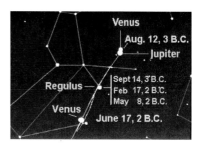

astonishing distance of *35 arc seconds*. To all but the sharpest of sight, for
about three hours before they drop below the western horizon, they are
joined into a magnificent bright single star, probably also made larger by the
lens of the atmosphere near the horizon (just like the Moon can look many
times larger near the horizon). Bullinger writes that the star of Bethlehem,
attested to by ancient authors, had to be "a new star":

> There can be little doubt that it was *a new star*. In the first place a new
> star is no unusual phenomenon. In the second place the tradition is well
> supported by ancient Christian writers. One speaks of its "surpassing
> brightness." Another (IGNATIUS, Bishop of Antioch, AD 69) says,
> "At the appearance of the Lord a star shone forth brighter than all the
> other stars." IGNATIUS, doubtless, had this from those who had
> actually seen it! PRUDENTIUS (4th century AD) says that not even the
> morning star was so fair. Archbishop TRENCH, who quotes these
> authorities, says "This star, I conceive, as so many ancients and moderns
> have done, to have been a new star in the heavens." [96]

To the common observer, this conjunction would be remarkable and
would certainly fill that description. In fact, the *Starry Night* program
indicates that it apparently remains faintly visible well into the following
morning (although beyond Palestine's visibility).

Jesus has now been born and the Creator God is the Infant at the breast
of Mary.

This conjunction occurs 24 hours before *Tammuz* 17 begins, a day of mourning for the Jew: on this day Moses descends Mount Sinai to discover Israel worshipping the golden calf; it also remembers the final weeks before the destruction of Solomon's Temple in 586 BC, and it is the day that begins the final three weeks before the destruction of Herod's Temple in 70 AD.[97] Already at His birth is the "pre-confirmation" of Jesus' prophecy that

> an hour is coming when neither on this mountain nor in Jerusalem will you worship the Father … an hour is coming, and now is, when the true worshipers will worship the Father in spirit and truth, for such the Father seeks to worship him.   John 4:21, 23

Elsewhere in the Universe

As the Sun highlights Gemini ("the Age of the Fall"), Mercury and Mars have just met in conjunction (June 5) in Cancer ("the Age of Creation"). The sin of "the Fall" is rebellion, and rebellion is the cause of the destruction of the temples, yet the situation is not hopeless: He Who will battle for creation, for a new heaven and a new earth, and for a new worship of God, now sleeps in Mary's arms.

B. "[He] Made Himself Empty, Taking a Servant's Nature, Being Made in Man's Likeness" *Philippians 2:7*

1. Conception or Birth?

A startling thought suggests itself. We get very excited about Christmas – and so we should, since this birth is the revealing of God's invasion into humanity, in celebration for which the angels tear aside the very curtain of heaven (a most unique event in itself!). Yet the birth is really only secondary. The more extraordinary event is the *conception*, where an almost invisible single cell – a fertilized egg – "contains" the Great Almighty Creator God, the Son. So if the actual miracle is the conception, should and does the Ballet of the Stars take notice of this greater occasion? If so, how does the time of gestation – conception to birth – fit into the Ballet?

The average length of human gestation is 266 days. Often 280 days is assumed, but that counts from the last menstrual period to birth, and since the egg cannot be fertilized until it is released from the ovary, the fourteen days after the start of the last period cannot be included.

Counting from August 12, 3 BC (first Venus-Jupiter conjunction) to May 8, 2 BC (last Jupiter-Regulus encounter), there is a total of 269 days, a startlingly close match, however there still is a three-day difference. Why should these days be significant? It could suggest a late birth; however, it may also point to something prior to the release of the egg from the ovary.

Normally conception is when *the seed of man*, the male sperm, (with 23 chromosomes) unites with the egg (with 23 chromosomes), bringing together the required 46 chromosomes that define a person's human body, but there is no such human father involvement for Jesus. How and when does He get the "other half" of the needed chromosome code? Truly, it could just "appear" at the right time. Or – when the egg itself is forming, in a process that actually starts from *Mary's* birth, rather than separating into a half chromosome content, it somehow retains the full 46 chromosomes. It forms as a "fertilized" egg, with the "other half" of the chromosome count also supplied by Mary, and therefore He is indeed truly *"the seed of the woman"* [Genesis 3:15].

There is an additional problem, though, since the "Y" chromosome which determines the male gender exists nowhere in a woman's body, one of the two female "X" chromosomes must be changed into a "Y" – the reversal of when God takes the rib of man and changes the "Y" chromosome to an "X", thereby forming the woman Eve [Genesis 2:21-2].

What is the event that the conjunction of August 12 appears to mark? Gabriel announces that Mary "*will* conceive" [Luke 1:31] – it has not happened yet. Although the human egg stands ready, the chromosome change must happen, and the unique combination of human and God also must happen. Three days before the egg is released from the ovary, Jehovah steps in, God the Son comes into human flesh, and a Baby Boy will be born.

2. The More Complete Picture

As we consider the length of time, why should we stop at the conjunction on May 8th? If we count the days from the Venus-Jupiter conjunction on August 12, 3 BC to the remarkable second Venus-Jupiter joining on June 17, 2 BC, it is *exactly* 269 + 40 days.

> A woman who has conceived and gives birth to a son will be unclean for seven days, just as she is unclean during the days of her monthly impurity. On the eighth day the flesh of his foreskin shall be circumcised. For thirty-three days she shall remain in the Blood of her cleansing; she shall not touch any holy thing, and she shall not enter the sanctuary until the days of her cleansing are fulfilled.   Leviticus 12:2-4

7 days to the circumcision plus 33 more days – 40 days is the period of "purification" for a woman who has just given birth to a male baby, at the end of which, according to Luke, Jesus is presented in Jerusalem in *the Temple*:

> When the eight days[98] were fulfilled in order to circumcise Him, His Name was called 'Jesus,' the angel had called Him before He was conceived in the womb. Now when the days of their purification were fulfilled according to the law of Moses, they brought Him to Jerusalem to present Him to the Lord.   Luke 2:21-22

269 plus 7 days (the eighth day) to Jesus' Circumcision has its place (to be discussed shortly), while the "33 days" also catches the eye, since Jesus' life on this earth spans "about" 33 years.

3. The Golden Parentheses

On August 12, 3 BC, a masculine Venus joins the New King, Jupiter; and on June 17, 2 BC, it is a feminine Venus joining Jupiter. In the first conjunction, Jesus (Jupiter) joins with human flesh (masculine Venus), in the second, Jesus is now at His mother (feminine Venus)'s breast; in the first He "empties" Himself [Philippians 2:7], "*leaving*" the throne of His Father [Ephesians 5:31-32], now in the second He is presented *before* the throne of His Father as the Seed of the woman.

This forms "the Golden Parentheses," an overview of Jesus' birth. Inside "the Parentheses," the feasts occurring at the conjunctions of Jupiter and Regulus describe the details of what Jesus is about and what He will do. As well, there is what could be in the heavens a "real-time" mirror/miming of what is happening on the earth.

Although the Magi have *some* of the *"HIS-Story"* through the prophecies, we have the advantage of knowing the full *Story* and therefore know even more fully what the meaning is to the Ballet of the Heavens. As best as can be determined, this Ballet has never occurred before – especially this convergence between the stars and planets hung at creation with the festival year commanded 1500 years prior to Jesus' birth –, and probably will not again. The Ballet cannot be mere happenstance, yet it does happen – now, at this place, at this time within world history. "In the fullness of time," the planets and the stars, for the first and only time, dance their message so that even "the heavens declare the Glory of the Lord."

4. Birth of Jesus – a scenario

Obviously the following is conjecture – because on this earth we will never know. And even if the interpretation is correct, there is no guarantee that what is happening in the sky is mirroring events presently happening on the earth: they could be predictive, real-time, or a recap of what has just happened. Because the star that led the Magi *is* real-time, it seems reasonable that the sequence within "the Golden Parentheses" is also a real-time declaration of what our Creator is doing for our salvation, but the reader can believe what seems best to him/herself.

1/ Aug 12, 3 BC – Morning Stars Jupiter and Venus (masculine) conjunction

The bright Morning Star (Jupiter), the New King, "His Star" – as the Magi refer to it – is at His rising. There is something afoot, something wonderful, in which human flesh (represented by the masculine Venus) joins the God-nature of "the Son" (represented by Jupiter, just as Saturn represents "the Father"). The month this conjunction begins is a call to prepare for the coming of the Lord.

2/ Aug 28-31, 3 BC – Mercury visits Venus

The messenger (Mercury) Gabriel meets with the masculine Venus, here representing "God the Son" (since the actual incarnation has not yet occurred), before being sent before Him to Mary.

3/ Sept 4, 3 BC – Mercury enters Virgo
Sept 5, Venus enters Virgo
Sept 6, Jupiter is eclipsed by an almost new Moon as it rises at 3:02 AM; it emerges at 4:45 AM
   Regulus rises at 3:12 AM, is eclipsed at 3:48 AM not long before Sunrise

Gabriel announces the breath-taking news, not only of the birth of the Messiah, but that Mary will be His mother.

The angel answered her, "The Holy Spirit will come upon you, and the power of the Most High will overshadow you; therefore Holy One that is born from you will be called the Son of God."   Luke 1:35

4/ Sept 9, 3 BC – The Moon becomes New (New Mother)
Sept 10, 3 BC – Rosh HaShanah
   The Head of the Year and *The Last Trump*
Sept 11, 3 BC – Revelation 12:1-2
   Rosh HaShanah's second day
Sept 14, 3 BC – Jupiter joins Regulus 1
   The Sabbath of the Return
Sept 19, 3 BC – Yom Kippur
   Day of Atonement and *The Great Trump*
Sept 24, 3 BC – Sukkoth – *The Festival of the Booths*
   The family in their stable/booth are visited by the seven shepherds.

During this time the Egg is radically altered, then is implanted in Mary's womb: the Creator, the Savior, the King, is *conceived in human flesh*, God has come to "tent" among humans as one of them. A "New Year" – Age – is beginning.

5/ Feb 17, 2 BC – Jupiter joins Regulus 2 – Purim

The Embryo Jesus is moving in the womb and, in month 5, the brain "explodes" in rapid growth.

6/ May 8, 2 BC – Jupiter joins Regulus 3 – Pentecost
The Festival of Harvest/First Fruits, The First Trump

As the end of Month 8 arrives, the Embryo Jesus has all necessary systems now developed – "the First Fruit" – , he could be born at any time during the coming last month, with very good chances for survival. However, He spends this next month getting "beefed up," which simply enhances the Baby's chances of survival after birth.

7/ June 6, 2 BC – Jupiter, Venus and Regulus mass in Leo;
New Moon *(not in sight of Palestine)*
passes Venus *(2 am morning)*
passes Regulus *(noon)*
passes Jupiter *(9 pm evening [7th])*

Mary and Joseph are likely enroute to Bethlehem. She is experiencing severe contractions.

8/ June 10, 2 BC – Jesus is born

269 days from Sept 14, 3 BC brings us to June 10th: Jesus' birth. Shepherds unquestionably are out in the fields. The Sun – representing the full Godhead and the Light that shines "in the darkness" [John 1:5] – is in Gemini (the "scene" of the Fall); Mars and Mercury are in Cancer (Good News for creation [Romans 8:19-22]: God has established His beachhead in the conflict for salvation); Saturn (the Star of David, of the Old Testament) is in Taurus (the constellation of judgment and renewal of mankind).

9/ June 17, 2 BC – Evening Stars Jupiter and Venus (feminine) are in an amazing conjunction

On the "eighth" day after birth (269 plus 7 days), Jesus is Circumcised and Named. Because Jesus is the full embodiment of Covenant,[99] therefore for the first time in all the history of the universe, God actually has Blood, and now He sheds *His own* Blood – His first Blood ever for salvation – in Circumcision, connecting Him to all who have already been joined within that Old Testament Covenant relationship, and receives His Name: "Jehovah saves." It is a most marvelous occasion and is most appropriately marked by the extraordinarily bright conjunction.

"The Golden Parentheses" is complete, although the end of *the Story* is not yet reached.

10/ July 20, 2 BC – The Sun and evening stars Jupiter, Mars and Mercury are in Leo, and (feminine) Venus is in Virgo

This would be the time of the actual presentation, after Mary's fulfilled 40 days after the birth, although this event does not occur within the "Golden Parentheses."

C. The Puzzle of September 11 and 14, 3 BC

1. Real-Time?

Diverse elements, from the "Ballet" of human history on earth to the coordinated Ballet of the Sky, from the yearning of mankind to the exuberant song of the angels, all contribute to mark the birth of the Holy Baby. Still there are some questions that remain. As one looks at the Ballet of the Sky, it seems to be "real-time," that is, that what is happening in the heavens is current to what is happening on earth. After all, especially for the Magi, the star that they follow has to happen *as* they follow it.

And yet, as is indicated in regard to Herod's death, timing seems to always be a problem. Revelation 12 (Virgo "clothed with the Sun" and the Moon at her feet) actually occurs (more or less) fairly frequently. However, the other celestial events going on in Leo seem to highlight that this one on

September 11, 3 BC, is indeed the one to notice. But exactly what does this event in Virgo tell us?

In first 5 verses of Revelation 12, the whole of Jesus' life is compressed: the scenario goes from the woman, to the birth, to the attempt to destroy the child, to Jesus' ascension. It is clear that Jesus does not die and does not ascend on this particular day in 3 BC. So, is the event to highlight Jesus' birth – or to highlight the real miracle, that of God the Son actually uniting with human flesh in the conception, since the birth merely *reveals* that miracle? Is it declaring something that is currently going on, or simply giving us the account of what has happened or will be happening perhaps shortly?

2. In the Sixth Month

> It came to pass in the days of Herod, king of Judea, a certain priest named Zacharias, of the division of Abijah. … Now it happened while he served as priest before God in the order of his division, that according to the custom of the priestly office, he was chosen by lot to burn the incense when he entered the temple of the Lord. … So it was, as soon as the days of his service were fulfilled, that he went to his home.
> Now after these days his wife Elizabeth conceived; and she hid herself five months, saying, "Thus the Lord has done to me, in the days when He looked to take away my disgrace among people."
> Now in the sixth month the angel Gabriel was sent from God to a city of Galilee named Nazareth, to a virgin engaged to a man whose name was Joseph, of the house of David and the virgin's name was Mary.　　　　　　　　　　　　　　　　　　Luke 1:5, 8-9, 23-27

"Now in the sixth month" [v 26] – if Month 7 (*Tishri*), day 2 (September 11, 3 BC, as perhaps suggested by Revelation 12) or day 5 (the 14th, as suggested by the first Jupiter-Regulus conjunction) is indeed the day of *conception*, then Gabriel's coming to Mary the week before (as Mercury's entering Virgo ahead of Venus might indicate) would indeed occur in Month 6 (*Elul*), "in the sixth month" – which fits Luke's "in the sixth month."

However, John the Baptist creates problems not just for Herod Agrippa,[100] but for us as well. *Elizabeth* also is "in *her* sixth month" [v 36] when Gabriel stands before Mary, after which Mary immediately heads over for a visit.[101]

Our problems begin here because John's father, Zachariah, is of "the division of Abijah." In I Chronicles 24, King David appoints 24 "divisions" of priests, each division serving a week in a set rotation. If the rotation starts in the first week of month 1 (*Nissan*, because God declares that *the Passover* month is always to be month 1 for Israel), then the rotation repeats a half year later approximately on month 7, week 1 (for the feast of *Rosh HaShanah*). The division of Abijah is the eighth in line, but since all priests are required or encouraged to serve together for the major festival weeks (*Passover, Pentecost*, and *Sukkoth* (Booths) [Deuteronomy 16:16]), his division would serve in either the ninth or the tenth week of the rotation. If so, Zachariah's duty falls at the beginning of month 3 (*Sivan*) and at the beginning of month 9 (*Keslev*).

If John the Baptist is conceived in the sixth month prior to Mary's Angel-visit, then this should occur during Month 1 (*Nissan* – March, 3 BC: month of *the Feast of the Firstborn* (the 14th) and of *the Passover* (the 15th to 22nd)). Since Zachariah serves in Month 3 and in Month 9, there is quite a gap of time between Gabriel's announcement to Zachariah that he will have a son in his and Elizabeth's old age, and the event actually occurring in Month 1.

3. Rotation Confusion

Darrell Pursiful identifies that the situation may be muddied in regard to the rotation of the priests:

> Twenty-four divisions each serving two weeks per year, plus the three additional weeks, makes up the fifty-one weeks of a standard Jewish year. (About every third year, an intercalary month was added to the Jewish year to bring it back into alignment with the solar year.) The questions are myriad:
> Did the priests serve the same two weeks every year, perhaps counting from the start of the year? ...
> Did the priestly rotation proceed strictly in accordance with the numbering of weeks, without reference to the calendar dates?
> What happened in leap years [when the extra month was added]? Did the priestly rotation simply continue apace, or was there some kind of special arrangement?
> Did the rotation schedule change at any point or was it consistent across the decades and centuries?[102]

As he alludes, since the calendar months are based on the lunar cycle (every month has and can only have one full Moon – there is no second, "blue" Moon), the year gets out of phase with the solar year. Around 600 BC, the Babylonians introduce a lunar Calendar system where the king of Babylon chooses when the extra month should be added. The Persians later standardize the addition to the 3rd, 6th, 8th, 11th, 14th, 17th and 19th years in a 19-year cycle.[103] If the rotation of priests follow a sequence that is begun at the start of each half year, how then is each extra month handled? Or if the rotation follows simply consecutively, then there is no way of knowing just when the "course of Abijah" would serve.

Also, what about the festival weeks in which all the priests are to serve? After all, the priests are not *all* going to, for instance, "burn the incense" at the same time – individuals must be chosen for the various tasks either as the priest *du jour,* or at least for a given time period, for instance, for three hours. One might expect a standardized priest-division rotation or possibly

94

a rotation determined by lot, in order to maintain the equality between the divisions. It is quite possible Zechariah does serve "in the order of his division, according to the custom of the priesthood" in that first month – and if Elizabeth conceives after Zechariah comes home, then when the angel speaks to Mary at the end of the sixth month, Elizabeth would be *just* starting her "sixth month."

We only assume that as soon as Zachariah goes home that Elizabeth immediately becomes pregnant, which may or may not be true. Although a gap of, for example, four months may seem like a long time, the Patriarch Abraham might have a word to add about a long wait between the promise of a son and its fulfillment.

4. The Course Rotation in 70 AD

At the destruction of the temple on August 5, 70 AD, Edersheim notes:

> In Taan.29a we have the notice, with which that of Josephus agrees (War vi.4.1,5), that at the time of the destruction of the Temple the course of Jehoiarib, which was the first of the priestly courses, was on duty. That was on the 9-10 Ab of the year 823 A.U.C., or the 5th August of the year 70 of our era. If this calculation be correct (of which, however, we cannot feel quite sure), then counting the courses' of priests backwards, the course of Abia would, in the year 748 A.U.C. (the year before the birth of Christ) have been on duty from the 2nd to the 9th of October. This also would place the birth of Christ in the end of December of the following year (749), taking the expression sixth month' in Luke 1:26, 36, in the sense of the running month (from the 5th to the 6th month, comp. Luke 1:24). But we repeat that absolute reliance cannot be placed on such calculations, at least so far as regards month and day. (Comp. here generally Wieseler, Synopse, and his Beiträge.).[104]

Although Edersheim is making the case for a December, 4 BC birth, he indicates that the course rotation does not follow the cycle where the first course always occurs in the first week of each half year – *Ab* (*Av*) is two months too soon. However, Darrell Pursiful states "We know from

Josephus that the first division, the division of Jehoiarib, was on duty when Jerusalem was besieged during the first week of April, AD 70 (*Nisan* 1-8, AM 3830)"[105] – which would identify the first course with the first week of the half year. This is a difference of 4 months between the two authors.

Edersheim provides a location for his assertion: Josephus' *Wars Of The Jews*, book VI, chapter 4, but that text only mentions the month of *Ab*, and has no mention in regard to the course of priests. Pursiful does not cite the location in Josephus for his claim.[106]

The long and short of this is that using the "course of Abijah" to identify the month when Zachariah serves, therefore the conception of John, and therefore the conception of Jesus, simply does not provide much by way of conclusive answers. Again it is up the reader to decide whether the Ballet of the Sky is mirroring events on earth or is merely summarizing for us "this thing that has come to pass, which the Lord has made known to us" [Luke 2:15].

VI. The Magi Come

A. The Magi's Journey:

"I see Him, but not now; I behold Him, but not near; a Star shall come out of Jacob; a Scepter shall rise out of Israel …"
                                                                    Numbers 24:17

1. August to September, 2 BC

After the Sun enters Virgo on August 22nd; on the 27th in Leo, a massing of Morning Stars Jupiter (again "at its rising" in the east on August 20), Mars, and Mercury lines up at the brink of entering Virgo: Jupiter and Mars are 13 arc

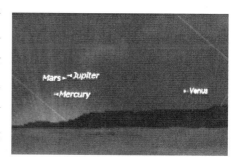

minutes apart, Mercury is 1½ degree away; and Venus is 9½ degrees to the side. Mercury enters Virgo the next day, along with the New Moon; Mars enters three days later (September 1); Jupiter enters ten days later (September 11). We are again back in the *Rosh HaShanah-Yom Kippur* time frame: September 1 (*Tishri* 3) coming two days after *Rosh HaShanah*, and September 11 (*Tishri* 13) falling between *Yom Kippur* and *Sukkoth*.

2. October 14, 2 BC

Meanwhile morning star (masculine) Venus slingshots up and then speeds down, entering Virgo on October 7 and passing Jupiter by about 1¾ degrees on October 14.[107] Although they are at a much greater distance than they had in Leo, still it is the third conjunction between them in a significant part of the sky within fourteen months. The Zoroastrian bible, the *Zend Avesta*, prophesies that a celestial event in Virgo[108] heralds the coming of the Jewish Messiah, Who is described as

> a king who would raise the dead and transform the world into a kingdom of peace and security. Interestingly, Zoroastrian traditions associated with the prophesied king said this king would come forth from the stock of Abraham. [The Encyclopaedia of Religion and Ethics, art. Zoroastrianism, XII.862–868].   Martin[109]

After the remarkable series of conjunctions that have come before, this third conjunction between Venus and "His star," Jupiter, is a likely candidate to fulfill this prophecy. Like sprinters awaiting the gun, this would induce the Magi to begin their journey to honor a King that has been wonderfully made known to them. As Jupiter moves westward, it points the way for the Magi to go.

3. The Caravan's Journey

Some legends speak of twelve Magi, but over time they have been narrowed to three because there are three classes of gifts given. It really does not matter, although to pay tribute to a King that they have traveled perhaps some 900 miles (from Ecbatana or Susa) to honor, with the best that the Silk Route to India and China has to offer, it does not seem likely that they are stingy with their representation. Their caravan would be extensive because crossing robber-infested desert and then plunging deep into enemy territory requires much in terms of supplies, as well as an elite guard of the *Cataphracti* (mounted cavalry). Travelling only 15 miles a day would get them to Jerusalem in two months.

4. December, 2 BC

Sweating the Visit – *Matthew 2:1-6*

Herod and his father have already run for their lives from the Persians, and now the Persian Cavalry have "crested the hills." All Herod has in Jerusalem is a guard – the actual Roman troops are stationed at Capernaum-by-the-Sea, and even then most of them are probably off fighting in the Homonadensian War. Even if the full complement were there, there is be nowhere near enough if Persia is on the march again.

So Herod, who has no qualms about torture and murder to protect his throne, has to swallow his pride and be on his diplomatic best when the Magi request the one "*born* King of the Jews." No doubt the Magi know this is a calculated insult to the one who has had to bribe, fight and siege his way to the throne and who knows that God says that the throne belongs only to the descendents of David – clearly the Magi (with their cavalry) have come to support "the real King." Betraying this understanding, Herod himself asks the chief priests and scribes where the *Messiah*, the *Christ*, is to be born – and in the ensuing account, he will set himself even against Jehovah in order to protect his throne.

On the other hand, Jerusalem always gets sieged in the ping-pong game of control between Rome and Persia. If Herod does anything foolish, there would be war – again – and there would be a siege, probably two – again. And even if he plays his hand skillfully (he does), who knows what repercussions he would later take out on the city anyway? Jerusalem is not feeling too happy about all this either.

Perhaps it is surprising that the dramatic celestial events of the months before are never noticed by the keepers of the prophecies in Palestine. No matter – they are sent back to the Word of God to find an answer to the

Magi's "Where?" and in Micah it is in Bethlehem where "The One to be Ruler in Israel, whose goings forth are from of old, from everlasting" [5:2] is to be found. How interesting that in spite of all this, the priests and scribes still show not even curiosity in regard to the Messiah so predicted by the prophesy they relay to these travelers.

December 25 – On the Road Again – Matthew 2:9-10

> When they heard the king, they departed; and behold, the star which they had seen in its rising [or the east] went before them, until it came and stood over where the Child was. When they saw the star, they rejoiced with exceedingly great joy.

There is no indication that the star had been obscured and only now becomes visible again. It is just that they had assumed that having reached the palace, their journey was done. Now that they are back on the road again, Jupiter is there, still moving before them – which they take as an affirmation that they are still on the right track. Then Jupiter stops between December 25-29 at what might be regarded as at the breast of Virgo (the upper third of the constellation), which would be fitting for the Child of perhaps 6½ months of age.

"Standing over the place" may refer to "dropping the perpendicular of a star." Jupiter's highest point (at 6:30 AM, an hour before sunrise) is about 68 degrees (out of 90 degrees) from the south horizon. Using simple geometry, one can draw a line from the star to the earth, which, from Jerusalem, points to Bethlehem. Possibly triangulation is then used to determine if indeed that town is to be their destination.[110] Also note:

> There is a beautiful tradition which relates how, in their difficulty, on their way from Jerusalem to find the actual spot under the *Zenith* of this star, these Magi sat down beside David's "Well of Bethlehem" to refresh themselves. There they saw the star reflected in the clear water of the well. Hence it is written that "when they saw the star they rejoiced with

exceeding joy," for they knew they were at the very spot and place of His appearing whence He was to "come forth."   Bullinger[111]

Since the planets follow the same track as the Sun which gets no higher than the Tropic of Cancer on the earth, one will therefore not see them in Palestine directly overhead (although Venus can sometimes get pretty close), so possibly this legend is the fabled version of the use of a well in terms of triangulation.[112]

Ultimately, it is not clear as to what "standing over the place" really means, and, other than a confirming sign, it is questionable how essential it is to the Magi anyway, since they already know that Bethlehem is the place of prophecy.

Celebrating Jesus' birth really does not matter in terms of how correct to the day we are, but there seems to be a precedent perhaps not in that the birth occurs on this date, but that the Magi are worshipping the infant King at this time.

Other Connections

It is the time of the winter solstice – when the Sun has also stopped its motion, soon to be "reborn" as the days lengthen and light triumphs over darkness. Although the Romans later have *The Feast of Saturnalia* to celebrate this transition, William Tighe asserts that there is in fact no evidence for a pagan observance of December 25 prior to Emperor Aurelian's decree.[113] Even so, early Christians recognize the symbolism of the returning Sun in light of the Malachi 4:2 prophecy of the Messiah, the Sun of Righteousness, Who "will arise with healing in His wings."

Hanukah (the Festival of Lights or *Feast of Dedication* [John 10:22]), celebrates when the Maccabees retake Jerusalem after the horror of Antiochus IV's rule, and desiring to rededicate the temple, the priests burn what is left of the holy oil, which should only last one day but miraculously lasts eight days. It is a fitting celebration for Jewish Christians to also celebrate the Messiah Who is the Light of the World [John 8:2] as well as remembering the parable of the wise virgins who have enough oil to trim their lamps at the coming of the Bridegroom [Matthew 25]. In many years *Hanukah* and Christmas often come close to each other, but unfortunately not in 2 BC. This is one of those years where the months are so out of phase that an extra month must be added in the coming February. Therefore *Hanukah* (*Keslev* 25)[114] starts on November 22, 2 BC.[115]

Elsewhere in the Universe

Morning Star (masculine) Venus and Mars are in Scorpio, which if it is indeed a sign of Satan and his power of sin and death, means that as these first Gentiles also come to worship Jesus, the battle with Satan is already engaged. These two planets are actually at the feet of Ophiucus as He is stepping on the head of Scorpio, which recalls Genesis 3:15's prophecy to the Serpent: "I will put enmity between you and the woman, and between your seed and her Seed; He shall bruise your head, and you shall bruise His heel" – as the earthly Jesus will indeed struggle with the Serpent of old.

Mercury, meanwhile, is in Sagittarius, the constellation accenting the "Chief Ancestor" and two-natured Chiron who gives up his immortality to die. The Sun is highlighting Capricorn, the combination of the Fish and the goat (the animal which figures so prominently in *The Day of Atonement* sacrifices – an atonement which will be for *all* the world).

Great Humility

The powerful Magi have gone to the palace in Jerusalem where one would expect to find a royal Baby. Now they find themselves in a mud brick hovel of a town (well, maybe not that bad, but still something quite out of their normal "orbit"). All that they know is that a Baby has been born. They do not know His parents. They do not know even where to start looking. The great and powerful Magi must go door-to-door like beggars to get information on an event they only vaguely know about. Just *how many* babies were born in the last year and a half? And if they did find Him, how would they know?[116]

Finally, perhaps one person recalls some "drunken shepherds" who did not see pink elephants, they claimed to have seen angels, and they made a lot of noise as they went back to their fields. Perhaps another thought they babbled about a Child in a manger. Someone recalls that a Child *was* born in a manger, but the family, naturally, is no longer in the stable. A helpful person suggests that the father may be a carpenter.

Finally they find a young Child, Who was born in a manger, Who was visited by shepherds, Who was announced by angels – but it is a Child from simple peasant folk. Quite possibly everything that they had expected has to be thrown away in order to discover God's Gift to mankind.

Their gifts to honor this King are the very best that world trade could offer, since the Persian Empire controls the Silk Route to India and China. They have brought gold and frankincense, the gifts that are prophesied in Isaiah 60:6, and myrrh, a perfume of royalty [Esther 2:12; Psalm 45:8; Proverbs 7:17].

5. Faith

Throughout the Old Testament there are many examples of where God confirms a person's faith only *after* they have put that faith in action. A notable example is when God calls Moses, He states: "I will be with you; and this shall be the Sign to you that I have sent you: *when you have brought the People out from Egypt,* you shall serve God on this mountain" [Exodus 3:12] –

God's proof is after the fact, when Moses discovers the successfulness of his faith, that God confirms it as His Sign.

The Magi, non-Jews, have made a journey into the unknown by a faith dictated by God's Word, through His prophecies and through His footprints in creation, and have discovered Jesus. Only *now*, after they have worshipped the Object of their journey, does God confirm their faith by speaking to them through an angel, instructing them to return by a different route.

B. Massacre of the Innocents

How long do the Magi stay after their visit with Jesus? Admittedly the nightlife in Bethlehem probably leaves much to be desired, but it also takes a few days to prepare for the journey back. Perhaps it is as they are leaving, that the angel comes to Joseph, telling him to take the family to Egypt, and by night they leave [Matthew 2:3-14].

Likely it is after a few days when Herod realizes that the Magi are not coming back. He has already determined to kill the Threat to his and his sons' throne, but now this requires a change in plan, since he has no idea Whom the Magi visited. Powerless to go after these "Wise Men" with what little troops that he has, to compel an answer from them, he also must be careful to not act too soon, lest they discover he has killed the King they have just traveled 900 miles to honor and the Persians respond with hostility, since he and his sons might not survive another war with them. So he waits until they are well on their way, perhaps a few days more, and then he strikes.

Sixteen days after December 25, 2 BC, a "Blood Moon" – a total, red eclipse – happens on January 10, 1 BC, beginning about 2 AM, reaching totality about 3:30 AM; the Moon emerges at about 6 AM and sets at about

7:30 AM. The bloody eclipse may mirror the blood of the two-year-old-and-under males of Bethlehem and its districts, whom Herod kills in order to protect his throne [vv 16-18], as "Rachel [is] weeping for her children" [Matthew 2:18].[117] The next eclipse signals Herod's own death a year later.

C. Herod's Eclipse

The December 29, 1 BC, partial eclipse, visible to the populace at Moonrise after Sunset, foreshadows Herod's own death (see earlier in this study in regard to the *Megillat Taanit* [Scroll of Fasts]). Herod has been suffering from a very rare and most painful disease, and after the eclipse, there is a turn for the worse in the last stages of the disease. He becomes frantic for a remedy to ease his suffering and bring healing. He orders what he intends will be the deaths of all the elders of the Jews. Herod dies on *Shevat* 7 (January 21), 1 AD. Because it has been a year since the Magi's visit, the Holy Family is safely dwelling in Egypt.

VII. The Ballet of the Sky, Part 2

A. Sing, O heavens, for Jehovah has done it! ... For Jehovah has redeemed Jacob, and glorified Himself in Israel.
Isaiah 44:23

The Not-so-Final Act

Approximately 33 years later, the Ballet, although much more subdued, continues. As mentioned earlier when establishing the date-vicinity of the birth of Jesus and the death of Herod, the best alternative for the crucifixion occurring on a Friday is *Nissan* 14 (April 3), 33 AD.

As the Ages Change, so do the Covenants

The Sun is in "the heart of" Aries (the Ram/Lamb, the Sign of Israel) as the culmination of Covenant and the fulfillment of the history and the sacrifices of the Old Covenant is reached. The morning star (masculine) Venus is in the center of Pisces as the Christian Age is dawning, and His messenger, Mercury, is with Him for the next 10 days before it enters Aries (the sign of Israel and the Jews). Evening stars Jupiter and Mars (later in conjunction on April 19) – the New King at war – is found in Gemini (the Sign of the Fall and of the promise to crush the head of the Serpent) on this day of Jesus' death.

Evening star Saturn (the Old King, the Creator, Jehovah of the Old Testament) is in Cancer (the Sign of Creation). Why *here* at Jesus' crucifixion? Perhaps it signals the beginning of the restoration of creation, as Paul describes,

> For in earnest expectation, creation expectantly awaits the revealing of the sons of God. For creation was subjected to aimlessness and

107

corruption, not voluntarily, but because of Him Who subjected it in hope; because the creation also will be freed from the slavery of corruption into the freedom of the Glory of the children of God. For we know that the whole creation groans and travails together until now.

Romans 8:19-22

The *Passover* Lamb – the Portal to Life

Of all the festivals particularly commanded by the Lord which are involved in the gestation and birth of Jesus, the one prominent omission is *the Passover* – and it has its role to fulfill now. This feast has a powerful message to its participants: while Israel is in Egypt and is helpless in the throes of slavery, Jehovah provides a miraculous redemption to free them not just from the Egyptians, but also from death. However it comes at the cost of an innocent victim, the lamb whose Blood is smeared on the doorway's two sides and top lintel of the house, making the door literally a doorway of Life. It is the *Sign* of Covenant [Exodus 12:13], the mark to all, even to the messenger of death, that these People belong to Jehovah Himself. It is the picture of Jesus: "I am the Door. If anyone enters by Me, he will be saved …" [John 10:9].

Not a bone of the lamb is to be broken [Exodus 12:46; Numbers 9:12; see Psalm 34:20; John 19:36], cooked for a people ready to travel immediately. To roast it whole [Exodus 12:9], Justin Martyr (c. 165) states that two wooden spits have to be placed at right angles to each other, stretching the lamb out on a cross.

There are two and three-quarter million people in Jerusalem now at this *Passover*, with some 256,500 lambs that must be slain before that evening.[118] To sacrifice that many lambs on a *Friday* when the lambs must be roasted *before* the *Sabbath* begins (since cooking is not allowed on a *Sabbath*), they must start "half an hour after noon" (that is, during the "sixth hour")[119], and for the next two hours, the lambs die.

108

The Apostle John records that as Pilate presents Jesus to the crowd, it is "about the sixth hour" (noon) [John 19:14]. Easily it is a half hour as Jesus is led away to Golgotha and is crucified – just as the Passover lambs are being slain. As His cousin, John the Baptist, announces at the beginning of Jesus' ministry, "Behold, the Lamb of God that takes away the sin of the world" [John 1:29].

Darkness

Not only do the Gospel writers speak of a darkness and an earthquake while Jesus hangs on the cross, secular writers do as well. Phlegon (quoted earlier) speaks of a "greater and more excellent eclipse" darkening the Sun, where the stars are visible in the sky. The duration is too short lived to be, for instance, dust thrown into the sky by an eruption of sorts. If an asteroid causes it, it must be very large, and if so, then passing so close to the earth, it might also cause the recorded earthquakes.

It cannot be caused by the Moon, since the Moon is on the other side of the earth, about to be eclipsed itself. Rick Larsen[120] in his DVD presentation has a video clip where *if one is standing on the Moon*, the Earth eclipses the Sun, and as Phlegon points out, Aries the Ram becomes visible with the darkened Sun – a "black hole" – where its heart would be, indeed visible from Jerusalem. As Jesus and the lambs are dying, "the Supreme Father" (the Sun) turns His face from His beloved Son, His sacrificial Lamb, reflecting

> About the ninth hour Jesus cried out with a loud voice, saying, "Eli, Eli, lama sabachthani?" that is, "My God, My God, why have You forsaken Me?"
> Matthew 27:46

We really have no idea what causes the darkness. As the angels pull aside the curtain of heaven for the Birth, perhaps they close the curtain for the Death. Ultimately we will have to wait until heaven to ask what its cause was. If it still matters.

A Blood Moon

The full Moon is in "the Scales of Justice," Libra, and it is another "Blood Moon" (although not total) eclipse occurring between 5 and 8:30 PM, not visible to Jerusalem until the tail end just rises at 8 PM at sundown, the start of the *Sabbath*. Reflected in the heavens, this is when Joseph of Arimathea and the others are taking Jesus' Body from the cross, doing a hurried preliminary preparation of it, and then hastily placing it in a nearby empty tomb before sundown. The Moon also reflects Simeon's prophecy to Mary, "yes, a sword will pierce through your own soul also" [Luke 2:35].

The Resurrection

Being the third day later, not much has changed in the heavens for the Resurrection. But then, that kind of message cannot be revealed by the stars. It is antithetical to fallen nature. Nature has no equipment to describe a true resurrection. It is something that can only be *announced* to us.

In regard to the festival year, of interest is that, although *"the Festival of the First Fruits"* is indeed linked to the *Pentecost* celebration in Numbers 28:26, in Leviticus 23:11 there is also apparently a "first" of the First Fruits ceremony that occurs on *the day after Passover* (*the Passover* is referred to as "the *Sabbath*"), which allows the Israelite to now eat from the grain as it is harvested [v 14]. When Jesus dies in 33 AD, the next day is a double *Sabbath* – both *Passover and* Saturday (the normal *Sabbath*) –, and He rises on *the day following "the Sabbath."*

On this day when the Israelite can begin to eat of the harvest, it is also the day when the risen Jesus is known to the Emmaus disciples in the

"Breaking of Bread" [Luke 23:30-31, 35], which becomes the way that the early disciples refer to Holy Communion [Acts 2:42, 46; 20:7; I Corinthians 10:16]. So as Jesus' People now follow His instructions, "Take and eat, this is My Body given for you" every Sunday following, they participate in the First Fruits of the Resurrection, which gives the frame of reference to Paul's words:

> But now Christ, raised from the dead, is the First Fruits of those who sleep. ... But each in his own order: the First Fruit Christ, then those who are Christ's at His coming.   I Corinthians 15:20, 23

The Ascension and Pentecost

For the Ascension on May 14, the Sun is now in Taurus (perhaps the Light dawning for the spirits in prison from the days of Noah [I Peter 3:18-20]). The morning star (masculine) Venus is in Aries (for those of God's People, "when they look on Him Whom they have pierced, they shall mourn for Him, as one mourns for an only child, and weep bitterly over Him, as one weeps over a first-born" [Zechariah 12:10]). The evening stars Mercury and Jupiter are in Gemini (there is Good News for those who are in the bondage of sin and death [Hebrews 9:15-16], "we have a great High Priest Who has ascended to the heavens" [Hebrews 4:14-15]). Mars and Saturn are in Cancer (perhaps reflecting the war between the Spiritual nature and our old nature that Paul speaks of in Romans 7:14-25).

Ten days later, for *Pentecost*, the birthday of the Church, Mercury and Jupiter are now in conjunction in Gemini – indeed the Good News is powerfully revealed for all who are affected by sin and death.

B. Forty Years Later

On August 4, 70 AD, there is a grand reunion of the Sun, morning star (masculine) Venus, evening stars Jupiter, Mercury, and Regulus in Leo; Saturn (the "Old King," the Star of David, the Star of Israel) is in the constellation of Libra, "holding" "the Scales of Justice"; and Mars is in the constellation of rebellious humanity, Gemini. It is *Av (Ab)* 9. It is the day that the rebellion of the Jews culminates in Rome's destruction of Jerusalem and of Herod's Temple.

It is about 40 years from the beginning of Jesus' ministry. Throughout the Bible, "40" identifies a time of preparation and purification, for example, Jesus' fasting for 40 days before Satan's temptation, even Mary's 40 days of purification before she could present the Baby Jesus in the Temple. However, unlike the 40 years in the wilderness which bring God's People into submission to His will, this 40-year refining time instead only more firmly exposes their rebellion.

Three years later, on *Nissan* 15 (April 10), 73 AD, *Passover - 40 (Hebrew[121]) years to the day after Jesus' death* -, the Jewish fortress at Masada falls to the Romans, and although the *People* of Israel do continue, the *nation* of Israel ceases for almost 1,900 years. This time Jupiter (Jesus) holds "the Scales of Justice" (Libra); the morning star (masculine) Venus is in Pisces, the Sun is again in Aries, while the messenger Mercury stands straddling Pisces and Aries; Mars is in Virgo; and Saturn is in Sagitarius (the sign of the "Chief Ancestor," and of wisdom, and of giving up immortality for death).[122]

For the Jew, if this indeed represents the day after Jesus' death, what then shall be considered as the following day, "*the day after the Sabbath*," the day of the First Fruits, the day of the Resurrection? Paul in Romans 9-11 attests that there is a remnant who will return to the Lord.

For I do not wish you to be ignorant of this mystery, brethren, lest you be wise to yourselves, that hardness has happened to Israel in part until the fullness of the Gentiles comes in. So all Israel will be saved, since it is written: "The Deliverer will come out of Zion, and He will turn away ungodliness from Jacob; for this is the Covenant with them from Me, when I take away their sins." ... For if their rejection means the reconciliation of the world, what will their acceptance mean but life from the dead?   Romans 11:25-27, 15

This resurrection is not merely a restoration of the nation (which occurred in 1948), but this "resurrection" of Israel will be to their Covenant God and Savior.

VIII. The Curtain Falls

The Ballet is over. No, this is not THE end – that will come when the heavens are filled with the clouds of Glory, when *THE Last Trump* finally sounds, and we see the Lamb crowned on His throne – and actually *that* starts a whole new Ballet of its own. But the physical journey on earth of the Son of God in the flesh is done. We are privileged, as Kepler said it, to "think God's thoughts after Him."

It has been like *anamorphic art*,[123] which at first seems distorted, even chaotic, until it is seen from the required viewpoint, even just a pinhole – and then a very recognizable picture emerges as the perspectives fall into their proper places. The far-flung occupants of the universe, planets and stars light-years from each other, seemingly hurled in a distorted and chaotic way throughout creation, combine into a totally unique Ballet which can be recognized from the pinhole that is Earth, when we have the proper perspective in hand: *"HIS-Story,"* the Bible. What at first seems like "all that jumping around on stage," we now see as God's tracks in the sky, connected to the God-given key events and festivals of Israel, and discover that indeed, "the heavens declare the *Glory* of the Lord" [Psalm 19:1], that is, His goodness, grace, mercy, Covenant, steadfast Love (*Hesed*), faithfulness, forgiveness and justice.

Yes, the skeptic can say that all this is by chance, and that we merely read into it what we want. Perhaps. Yet the picture, its connections and its precision as seen in this Ballet, as something that occurs possibly only once throughout all time, yet occurs at *this significant point of time*, is very compelling. "Coincidence" becomes a profoundly pathetic word by which to dismiss it all. But, of course, that is always the choice of the reader.

We see astrology, not as it has become, but as it should be, not as a dictator of our lives but as a creature which bears witness to the activity of its Creator (as all creation, all science, even we, should); not where creation is a mechanized "influence" on our personalities but rather that it draws our attention to Him Who can and does do things impossible to our minds, Who accomplishes His will in the whole universe, yet Who can also be personally involved with each of us on this tiny planet.

> Where were you when I laid earth's foundations? Declare it, if you have the understanding! Who set its measurements – because you know! Or Who stretched the foundation string lines upon it? In what were its footings sunk and Who laid the cornerstone, when the morning stars sang together, and all the sons of God shouted for joy?   Job 38:4-7

At creation the morning stars sing, but when Jesus comes to "tent" among us, they dance, and it is a wonderful, exquisite Ballet.

Endnotes

[1] [http://www.reddit.com/r/todayilearned/comments/etg46/til_that_neither_snow_
nor_rain_nor_heat_nor_gloom/?sort=hot] (accessed 02/05/2011):
   … it actually came from the Persian Empire:
   http://en.wikipedia.org/wiki/United_States_Postal_Service_creed

> The United States Postal Service has no official creed or motto. Often falsely
> cited as such, "Neither snow nor rain nor heat nor gloom of night stays these
> couriers from the swift completion of their appointed rounds" is an inscription
> on the James Farley Post Office in New York City, derived from a quote from
> Herodotus' Histories (8.98), referring to the courier service of the ancient
> Persian Empire:
>> It is said that as many days as there are in the whole journey, so many are
>> the men and horses that stand along the road, each horse and man at the
>> interval of a day's journey; and these are stayed neither by snow nor rain
>> nor heat nor darkness from accomplishing their appointed course with all
>> speed. (trans. A.D. Godley 1924)

See… http://en.wikisource.org/wiki/History_of_Herodotus/Book_8

> 98. Nothing mortal travels so fast as these Persian messengers. The entire plan
> is a Persian invention; and this is the method of it. Along the whole line of
> road there are men (they say) stationed with horses, in number equal to the
> number of days which the journey takes, allowing a man and horse to each day;
> and these men will not be hindered from accomplishing at their best speed the
> distance which they have to go, either by snow, or rain, or heat, or by the
> darkness of night. The first rider delivers his dispatch to the second and the
> second passes it to the third; and so it is borne from hand to hand along the
> whole line, like the light in the torch-race, which the Greeks celebrate to
> Vulcan. The Persians give the riding post in this manner, the name of
> "Angarum."

[2] Hyam Maccoby

[3] Ernest L. Martin, *The Star that Astonished the World*, Chapter II: "Who Were the Wise
Men?", (all references to Martin's book were downloaded from
[http://www.askelm.com/star/] on 2/9/2011):

> Josephus said that it was shown in the "sacred writings that about that time one
> from their country [Judaea] should become governor of the habitable earth"
> [Josephus, *War* VI.xxi.3]. …
> Even the Romans were aware of the prophecies of Daniel. Suetonius in the
> early 2nd century said, "A firm belief had long prevailed through the east that it was
> destined for the empire of the world at that time to be given to someone who
> should go forth from Judaea" [Suetonius, *Vespasian*, 4]. The Roman historian
> Tacitus also said,
>> "The majority of the Jewish people were very impressed with the belief that it
>> was contained in ancient writings of the priests that it would come to pass that
>> at that very time, the east would renew its strength and they that should go
>> forth from Judaea should be rulers of the world" [Tacitus, *History*, V. 13].

117

Even the Roman Emperor Nero was advised by one or two of his court astrologers that it was prudent for him to move his seat of empire to Jerusalem because that city was then destined to become the capital of the world [Suetonius, *Nero*, 40].

4 Jona Lendering, "King Herod the Great," [http://www.livius.org/hehg/herodians/herod_the_great01.html] (accessed 01/9/2011). Matthew 1:17 identifies 42 generations from Abraham; Luke 3:23-38 lists Jesus as the 77th generation from Adam.

5 Martin, Chapter II, sub-heading "The Professional Role of the Magi," quoting from *The Encyclopaedia of Religion and Ethics*, art. Zoroastrianism, XII.862–868.

6 Josephus, *Jewish Antiquities*, XVII, vi, 4 [http://www.sacred-texts.com/jud/josephus/ant-17.htm] (all Josephus material was downloaded 2/9/2011):
But Herod deprived this Matthias of the high priesthood and burned the other Matthias, who had raised the sedition, with his companions, alive. And that very night there was an eclipse of the moon.

7 Darrell Pursiful's blog, "When Was Jesus Born? The Census," December 15, 2006, [http://pursiful.com/2006/12/when-was-jesus-born-the-census/]:
Tertullian states that censuses (plural) were conducted in Palestine around the time of Jesus' birth. There are two viable candidates for the census described in Luke 2. One is the census of 8 BC (the second of three censuses ordered by Augustus during his 41-year reign), documented by an inscription found at the temple of Augustus in Ankara, Turkey.

8 [www.versebyverse.org/doctrine/birthofchrist.html] (accessed 1/16/2011):
q. That the registration was not for the purpose of taxation is seen by the fact that as long as King Herod was alive, no taxes were paid to Rome - rather they were paid directly to Herod (immediately upon Herod's death, the Jews asked Archelaus [Herod's successor] to relieve them of excessive taxes [*Antiquities*, XVII, 205]). Had the Jews been paying taxes directly to Rome brought about by the census of Quirinius, this request would have been irrelevant. From 63BC to 47BC Judea was part of the province of Syria and paid tribute directly to Rome. From 47BC to 40BC Hyrcanus was the "ruler of the free republic" [*Antiquities*, XIV, 117], but the Jews still paid direct taxes to Rome. When Herod became king, however, the tribute to Rome ceased and Herod collected all the taxes. This continued until 6/7AD when direct taxation was again imposed in Judea [see P.C. Sands, *The Client Princes of the Roman Empire*, pps. 222-228].

9 *Ibid.*

10 Barry Setterfield ("THE CHRISTMAS STAR: Technical notes; PART 1: WHEN WAS JESUS BORN?", [http://www.setterfield.org/startechnical.html]), says that a world census is needed for Strabo to complete his map of the Empire with a commentary called "Geography," and that such censuses were a regular institution since 28 BC. Although Strabo is finished by 6 BC, Setterfield maintains that it takes six years to complete the census (until about 2 BC). For an empire that develops an efficient network of roads for rapid movement from place to place, that moves armies to the frontier in a matter of months, that clears the Mediterranean of pirates so that the only real concern for travel is favorable weather, and has already a number of censuses under

its belt, as well as a system of taxation, 6 years seems a bit ponderous and forced. This is especially when considering the census/oath of allegiance to which all members of the empire were to submit was initiated in 3 BC and "completed" by February 2, 2 BC – which is far more in character with the efficiency of the Roman governance.

When the census supposedly takes six years, is the census done sequentially through its provinces, rather than concurrently? It is likely that the edict would go out immediately to all the Roman appointed governors and legates within the empire the moment the edict is issued. In the 3-2 BC census/oath of allegiance, when 6,000 Pharisees refuse, it is Herod who fines them – here the local ruler appears to have the responsibility for completing the edict's demands. With a system of tax collectors already in place, who would already hold the tax rolls, it does not seem logical to conclude that a census would take six years to complete.

[11] Martin, Chapter 1, sub-heading: "The Glory of Rome"

[12] Martin, Chapter 1, sub-heading: "The Father of the Country"

[13] John P. Pratt, "Yet Another Eclipse"; also John Mosley (Program Supervisor, Griffith Observatory, Los Angeles, California), in "Common Errors in 'Star of Bethlehem' Planetarium Shows" [http://www.ldolphin.org/birth.html], following Dr. Ernest Martin, adds:

> An inscription from Paphlagonia in Asia Minor from 3 B.C. records an oath "taken by the inhabitants of Paphlagonia and the Roman businessmen dwelling among them ... The same oath was sworn also by all the people in the land at the altars of Augustus ..." Note that the common thread here is an oath of allegiance required of all the people, citizen and noncitizen alike, both in the empire and its provinces, for the purpose of establishing fealty. This oath was either ordered by Augustus at the time of his jubilee and completed that year (2 B.C.), or was conducted during the year prior to the jubliee (3 B.C.) and the results presented to him as part of the ceremonies.

Also: [Birth & Crucifixion Dates of Yeshu bar Miriam - The Order of Nazorean Essenes - essenes.net-index.php-Itemid=578&id=144&option=com_content&task=view] mention that an inscription in Asia Minor, dating from 3 BC confirm this census-oath.

[14] Josephus, *Antiquities*, XVII.ii.4

[15] Pursiful, "Census"

[16] *Ibid.*

[17] *Ibid.*

[18] The website: [http://star.wind.mystarband.net/bib/tiberius_timeline.html], lays out an apparent well-documented case for numbering from the beginning of the co-reign of Augustus. On the other hand, Murrell Selden ["The Date of Herod's Death: The Errors Corrected, " 11/15/95 (Revised 12/16/98)
[http://home.comcast.net/~murrellg/Herod.htm] believes that Tiberius' reign began on August 19, 14 AD, and that "in the fifteenth year" therefore spans 28-29 AD.

[19] [http://star.wind.mystarband.net/bib/tiberius_timeline.html]

[20] Nissan 15 (April 4), 33 AD minus 3 years ministry equals Nissan 15 (April 6), 30 AD; minus 30 years yields Nissan 15 (April 8), 1 BC. The Ballet of the Sky, later in this paper, suggests a birth of June 7, 2 BC, which would be a ten month difference.

[21] [http://star.wind.mystarband.net/bib/jesus_historicity.html#eusebius] quotes from Eusebius' *Chronicle, 202nd Olympiad* (c. 311 A.D. as preserved by Jerome), who quotes Phlegon.

[22] However, [star.wind.mystarband.net]:

> historians generally accept the 1st Olympiad to have been 776/5 B.C. (though this is not absolutely fixed)… Phlegon may have computed the year wrong (2nd year of 202nd Olympiad would give a consistent result) or the generally accepted date of the first Olympiad 776 B.C. may be in error (778 B.C. would give a consistent result). Further investigation is to be done.

Since the writer of [star.wind.mystarband.net] has his own ax to grind, promoting his own date, therefore he is quick to say that Phlegon must be wrong and the date moved to two years earlier.

[23] Mosley, "Common Errors":

> Tertullian (born about 160 AD) stated that Augustus began to rule 41 years before the birth of Jesus and died 15 years after that event. Augustus died on August 19, 14 AD, placing Jesus' birth at 2 BC. Tertullian also notes that Jesus was born 28 years after the death of Cleopatra in 30 BC, which is consistent with a date of 2 BC. Irenaeus, born about a century after Jesus, also notes that the Lord was born in the 41st year of the reign of Augustus. Since Augustus began his reign in the autumn of 43 BC, this also appears to substantiate the birth in 2 BC. Eusebius (264-340 AD), the "Father of Church History," ascribes it to the 42nd year of the reign of Augustus and the 28th from the subjection of Egypt on the death of Anthony and Cleopatra. The 42nd year of Augustus ran from the autumn of 2 BC to the autumn of 1 BC. The subjugation of Egypt into the Roman Empire occurred in the autumn of 30 BC. The 28th year extended from the autumn of 3 BC to the autumn of 2 BC. The only date that would meet both of these constraints would be the autumn of 2 BC.

[www.hope-of-israel.org/herodsdeath.html]:

> The evidence of history, archaeology and astronomy is now showing that Herod died in early 1 B.C. and that the Messiah was therefore born in 3/2 B.C. (regnal dating) – as confirmed by Irenaeus, Clement of Alexandria, Tertullian, Africanus, Hippolytus of Rome, Hippolytus of Thebes, Origen, Eusebius and Epiphanius.

Darrell Pursiful's blog [http://pursiful.com/2006/12/when-was-jesus-born-herods-death/]:

> According to Clement of Alexandria, Jesus was born in the twenty-eighth year of Augustus' rule of Egypt. This has to be dated from the battle of Actium, September 2, 31 BC. The Egyptian custom was to count the inaugural year of a ruler's reign as an accession year, with the next year being "year one." The Egyptian new year after the battle of Actium fell on August 31, 30 BC. By this reckoning, Augustus' 28th

year as ruler of Egypt would have run from Thot 1 (August 24), 3 BC to Thot 1 (August 24), 2 BC.

Darrell Pursiful. "When Was Jesus Born? Clement of Alexandria," December 19, 2006 [http://pursiful.com/2006/12/when-was-jesus-born-clement-of-alexandria/]:

> The earliest known discussion of the calendar date of Jesus' birth comes from Clement of Alexandria (Stromata 1:21), who writes: "From the birth of Christ, therefore, to the death of Commodus are, in all, a hundred and ninety-four years, one month, thirteen days." Using the Roman calendar, this works out to November 18, 3 BC. But this is a highly doubtful conclusion, affirmed by no other ancient source. More likely, Clement was using the Egyptian calendar, which did not make provisions for leap years. By that calendar, counting backwards from emperor Commodus' death on December 31, AD 192, an interval of 194 years (each exactly 365 days), one month (thirty days), and thirteen days yields a date of January 6, 2 BC. ...

> **Egyptian Traditions**

> If we reckon Augustus' reign from the Battle of Actium, September 2, 31 BC, when he put down his last rival, Antony, and if we count the accession year according to Egyptian custom, Augustus' twenty-eighth year on the Egyptian calendar lasted from August 24, 3 BC to August 24, 2 BC.

[24] Birth & Crucifixion Dates of Yeshu bar Miriam - The Order of Nazorean Essenes – [essenes.net-index.php-Itemid=578&id=144&option=com_content&task=view]. Also [http://www.wordiq.com/definition/Herod#Date_of_His_Death]:

> Another line of calculation centres around the age of Herod at the time of his death. Josephus says that he was about 70 years old. He says that at the time Herod received his appointment as governor of Galilee (which is generally dated 47 BC), he was 15 years old; but this has been understood by scholars to be an error, 25 years evidently being intended. (Jewish Antiquities, XVII, 148 [vi,1]; XIV, 158 [ix,2]). Accordingly, Herod's death occurred in 2 BC or 1 BC whereas Appianos would place it at 1 BC or 1 AD.

[25] As the *Starry Night* program shows, there are no other eclipses in 3-2 BC, nor in 1 AD are observable in Jerusalem.

[26] John P. Pratt, "Yet Another Eclipse":

> ... So why did Josephus include Herod's eclipse but no others?

> An obvious answer is that *the eclipse was widely observed* and then associated with the executions. If so, then *the eclipse occurred in the early evening*. Using this criterion, the eclipses of March 13, 4 B.C. and January 10, 1 B.C. are extremely unlikely because they both began the umbral phase more than six hours after sunset and hence would have only been seen by at most a few people. The eclipse of Sept 15, 5 B.C. began three hours after sunset, but that is also late.

> On the other hand, the eclipse of December 29, 1 B.C. fits this criterion very well. The full moon was nearly half eclipsed when it could first be seen rising in the east above the distant mountains about twenty minutes after sunset. ... It would not have been seen much before that time, even without the mountains, due to sky brightness. At first the eclipsed half of the full moon would have been invisible,

then it would have appeared dimly lit, and finally the characteristic reddening of the eclipsed portion would have become noticeable. The umbral phase continued for about an hour after first visibility. Note that a partial eclipse is more easily seen at moonrise than a total because totality delays first visibility (the entire moon is in the "invisible" portion) and the shape of the missing portion would have made it obvious that it was an eclipse, especially to the Judeans who used the moon to indicate the day of the month and who expected a full moon. Of the candidates to be Herod's eclipse, *the December 29, 1 B.C. eclipse was the most likely to have been widely observed.*

27 From [http://www.attalus.org/translate/taanit.html], which provides the translated text.

28 There are some who claim the date for Herod's death as *Shevat/Shebat* 2, Ernst Martin [Chapter IX, under heading "The Only Eclipse that Meets All Factors"] being one; however, Solomon Zeitlin gives the date as the 7th in his well known work, *Megillat Taanit as a source for Jewish chronology and history in the Hellenistic and Roman periods* [http://openlibrary.org/books/OL23318246M/Megillat_Taanit_as_a_source_for_Jewish_chronology_and_history_in_the_Hellenistic_and_Roman_periods]   From this site Zeitlin's book can be downloaded as a pdf of the scanned pages).

29 Aryeh Kasher and Eliezer Witztum, *King Herod: A Persecuted Persecutor* [Walter de Gruyter GmbH & Co. KG, Berlin, 2007], Pg 390:

> The killing of the sages and their students was an act so shocking that it earned Herod a lasting reputation as a bestial "killer of scholars"; for this reason, the date of his death is referred to as a day of celebration on which mourning, fasting, or eulogizing are prohibited.

30 Rabbi Moshe Lichtman, *Chanukah in Hashkafa and Halachah: Peninei Halacha on Chanukah*, Yeshiva University, Kislev 5771 [http://www.yutorah.org/togo/ chanuka/articles/Chanuka_To-Go_-_5771_Rabbi_Lichtman.pdf], pgs 13, 17]:

> The Sages also established holidays when the evil kings who persecuted them died: King YUanni on the 2nd of Shevat and King Herod on the 7th of Kislev. Many other dates are mentioned in *Megillat Ta'anit*. ...
> When Herod died, in 3757 (4 BCE), the sages established the day of his death – the seventh of Kislev – as a holiday.

31 According to the *Fourmilab Calendar Converter.*

32 As a side comment there seems to be confusion in regard to a fast that Josephus mentions in *Antiquities*, XVII, vi, 4:

> Now it happened, that during the time of the high priesthood of this Matthias, there was another person made high priest for a single day, that very day which the Jews observed as a fast. The occasion was this: This Matthias the high priest, on the night before that day when the fast was to be celebrated, seemed, in a dream, to have [sexual intercourse] with his wife; and because he could not officiate himself on that account, Joseph, the son of Ellemus, his kinsman, assisted him in that sacred office.

Some have interpreted that this fast occurs at the execution of the two rabbis, after which that night the eclipse preceeding Herod's death takes place. The passage does not say this – it only indicates that during this Matthias' term of office, that there is an occasion when a substitute has to stand in. Matthias is put into office during the conspiracy trial of Antipater according to *Antiquities*, XVII, iv, 2 and so Matthias' term of office spans at least a number of months, any time during which this fast could have occurred.

33 Josephus, *Antiquities*, XVIII, iv, 6

34 Jack Finegan, *Handbook of Biblical Chronology: The Principles of Time Reckoning in the Ancient Word and Problems of Chronology in the Bible*, rev. ed. (Peabody: Hendrickson Publishers, 1998), 298-301:

> In fact, however, already in the nineteenth century Florian Riess reported that the Franciscan monk Molkenbuhr claimed to have seen a 1517 Parisian copy of Josephus and an 1841 Venetian copy in each of which the text read "the twenty-second year of Tiberius." The antiquity of this reading has now been abundantly confirmed.
>
> In 1995 David W. Beyer [*Josephus Re-Examined: Unraveling the Twenty-Second Year of Tiberius, in Chronos, Kairos, Christos II*, edited by E. Jerry Vardaman (Macon: Mercer University Press, 1998)] reported to the Society for Biblical Liturature his personal examination in the British Museum of forty-six editions of Josephus's Antiquities published before 1700 among which twenty seven texts, all but three published before 1544, read "twenty-second year of Tiberius." Likewise in the Library of Congress five more editions read the "twenty-second year," while none prior to 1544 records the "twentieth year."

However, Kenneth F. Doig, *New Testament Chronology* (Lewiston, NY: Edwin Mellen Press, 1990). [http://www.doig.net/NTC04.html], Chapter 4: HERODIAN CHRONOLOGY:

> [Added note: * David Byer makes the case that Herod's departure from this life in the 20th year of the reign of Tiberius is an error for 22nd year, thus placing Herod's death in 1 BCE. The Basel edition of Antiquities, printed in Greek in 1544, uses the 20th year, and was soon accepted as the standard. Byer examined printed versions of Josephus in the British Library and Library of Congress, many of which were printed before 1544 and used the 22nd year. Based on the existence of these "22nd year" volumes he presumes by their early predominance that this is how Josephus wrote it over a millennium earlier. What is missing from his dissertation is an examination of any hand-written histories, with provenance, on which the printed versions were based. A search in Basil, the Vatican Library, etc. might have produced a more convincing data set. We are also missing any information on why 16th century scholars quickly abandoned the 22nd year in favor of the 20th years. Byer's research does not justify a shift to the 22nd year and 1 BCE death of Herod (unless you need to justify the errant 33 CE date for the Crucifixion of Jesus).]

35 Finegan, *Handbook of Biblical Chronology*, 298-301.

36 Selden, "The Date"

37 Martin, Chapter VII, sub-heading: "There Are Chronological Errors in Josephus"

38 Martin, Chapter VII, sub-heading: "The Anomalies of Josephus"; See also Ed Bromfield, [http://smoodock45.wordpress.com/2009/12/24/fixing-the-date-of-herod %E2%80%99s-death-part-3/]; also [http://www.wordiq.com/definition/Herod#Date_of_His_Death].

39 [www.visionvideo.com/pdf/ChronologyInformation.pdf], with no indication of author nor of any sources, however the observations made are echoed by many commentators.

40 See Ernest Martin's book, noted above. There is also quite a discussion between a "Joe Baker" and a "Tory" concerning historical dates in the forum "Re: Date of Herod's Death" beginning on "Wed May 9, 2007 08:27" at [http://disc.yourwebapps.com/discussion.cgi?disc=177754;article=8451;title=The%20A ncient%20Near%20Eastern%20Chronology%20Forum]. Other discussions: John P. Pratt, "Yet Another Eclipse"; Doig, *New Testament Chronology*, Chapter 4; also [http://star.wind.mystarband.net/bib/jesus_birthdate.html]; [http://pursiful.com/2006/12/when-was-jesus-born-the-census/]; Blessed Be The God Of Israel – [www.theendtimesobserver.org-archives-index.php-id=401]; [www.hope-of-israel.org/herodsdeath.html].

41 [http://star.wind.mystarband.net/bib/jesus_birthdate.html]:

Historically, the rainy season in Palestine begins with the early rains in the month of Heshvan (mid-October) and runs through Iyar (mid-May), with the heaviest rains mid season accounting for 70 percent of Bethlehem's annual rainfall and the latter rains in Nisan (see "Ancient Ecologies and the Biblical Perspective" by Edwin M. Yamauchi, *Journal of the American Scientific Affiliation* 32.4, Dec. 1980, 193-202). Temperatures in Bethlehem during the coldest months of Tevet and Shevat (mid December through mid-February) average 11-14 degrees Celsius (55°F) and reach lows of 1 degree Celsius (33°F) (see Bethlehem Municipality - Climate).

See Adam Clarke, *Commentary on the Bible*, Luke 2:8; Albert Barnes, *Notes on the Bible*, Luke 2:8; Jamieson, Fausset and Brown, *Commentary Critical and Explanatory on the Whole Bible*, Luke 2:8.

42 Darrell Pursiful, "When Was Jesus Born? The Date of Jesus' Birth?" December 17, 2006 [http://pursiful.com/2006/12/when-was-jesus-born-the-date-of-jesus-birth/]; see also Doig, *New Testament Chronology*, Chapter 4.

43 Herodotus, I, 101; Pliny, *Natural History*, V, 29; also Martin, Chapter II, sub-heading: "The Professional Role of the Magi":

There is a considerable amount of early information about the Magi of the east. We are told by the ancient historian Herodotus that they were originally one of the six tribes of the Medes, a priestly caste similar to the Levites among the Israelites. In their early history their occupation was to provide the kings of the Medes, Persians and Babylonians with what they considered to be divine information about the daily matters involving government affairs. Because of the high religious and political esteem accorded them by the peoples of the east, they were able in the 6th century B.C.E. even to overturn some royal powers.

44 Doig. Laert. IX, 7,2; Martin, Chapter II, sub-heading: "The Jews and the Magi":

124

Jews in the 1st century respected the Magi. The Jewish philosopher by the name of Philo, who lived in Alexandria, Egypt during the time of Jesus, spoke of the Magi with warm praise. Philo said they were men who gave themselves to the study of the laws of nature and that they contemplated on the divine perfections. To Philo they were worthy of being counselors of kings. [Philo, Quo. Probus Liber, 74.]

[45] Martin, Chapter II, subheading: "The Jews and the Magi":

The main occupation of the Magi was their interpretation of things they considered divine. They principally dealt with the evaluation of dreams, visions and astronomical signs. Astrological interpretation was of special importance to them. The temple of Belus in what remained of the city of Babylon was in their care [Diodorus Siculus, II.31; Ephraem, Syrus, II.488]. In particular, they were advisors to kings and princes and they were especially consulted regarding the destinies of kings [Diogenes Laertius IX.7.2]. The Parthian kings of the east had them as their advisors and they were the ones who performed the ceremonies at their coronations [Zondervan Pictorial Encyclopedia of the Bible, IV.34]. The Roman authors Cicero and Plutarch inform us that the Magi were the ones who instructed kings and princes in the east. Except in rare circumstances, only royalty were allowed to be initiated into their secret teachings and understandings [Strabo, XVI.762; Cicero, De.Divin., I.41].

[46] Philo, Quod Omn,. Prob. (74)

[47] Herodotus, III, 61 sq.

[48] Barry Setterfield, THE CHRISTMAS STAR [http://www.ldolphin.org/birth.html]:

But why did the Persian Magoi make such a perilous trip at all? There were 3 reasons. Firstly, the Hebrew prophet Daniel had been held in high regard in the Persian court. In Daniel 9, the Magoi had the prophecy of Messiah's sacrifice as a man cut off at age 35 (in the midst of his years). They knew that this event would occur 483 Babylonian years of 360 days after a specific decree. Backtracking 35 years gave a birth date for Messiah of 448 Babylonian years or 442 actual years after the decree. As It turned out, that decree was Issued by the Persian king Artaxerxes in his 20th year which was 445/444 BC. The Magoi consequently knew the time of Messiah's birth as around 3/2 BC on our Calendar.

[49] Some discussions on this prophecy can be found at: [http://www.bible.ca/ef/expository-daniel-9-24-27.htm]; [http://www.aboutbibleprophecy.com/weeks.htm]; [http://en.wikipedia.org/wiki/Prophecy_of_Seventy_Weeks]; [http://www.harvardhouse.com/Gabriel-to-Daniel_3.htm]; [http://www.harvardhouse.com/Gabriel-to-Daniel_3.htm]; [http://www.adventistbiblicalresearch.org/documents/Whendid70WksofDan9begin.html]; [http://en.wikipedia.org/wiki/Prophecy_of_Seventy_Weeks]

[50] About Bible Prophecy's "Daniel's Seventy Weeks prophecy: A detailed look at Daniel 9:24-27" [http://www.aboutbibleprophecy.com/weeks.htm]

[51] *ibid.*

[52] Since no day date is given, the date of *Nissan* 1 is simply assumed.

53 [http://www.gotquestions.org/seventy-sevens.html]:

As for our starting point, the Persian Emperor Artaxerxes Longimanus (who ruled Persia from 464-424 BC) issued the edict to rebuild Jerusalem sometime during the Hebrew month of Nisan in the 20th year of his reign, or 444 BC (Nehemiah 2:1-8). The month of Nisan fell between February 27 (Nisan 1) and March 28 (Nisan 30) of that year according to our modern Gregorian calendar.
  Now, 173,880 days from February 27 - March 28, 444 BC, lands us at March 24 - April 22, AD 33.

54 Sachiko Kusukawa, "Kepler and Astrology," Department of History and Philosophy of Science, University of Cambridge, copyright 1999. [www.hps.cam.ac.uk/starry/keplerastrol.html]

55 [http://dictionary.reference.com/browse/astrology]

56 Dr Kenneth G Negus, "Kepler's Astrology" – [cura.free.fr/docum/15kep/en.html]

57 Agnes M. Clerke, "Johannes Kepler, German mathematician, astronomer and astrologer (1571-1630)" – [www.1902encyclopedia.com/K/KEP/johannes-kepler.html]

58 Ann Lamont, "Johannes Kepler, Outstanding Scientist and Committed Christian" – [www.answersingenesis.org/creation/v15/i1/kepler.asp]

59 Negus, "Kepler's Astrology"

60 Check out the HuffPost's delightful tongue-in-cheek slideshow [http://www.huffingtonpost.com/2011/01/14/new-astrological-signs-_n_808635.html#s223555&title=Your_Entire_Personality] on how the apparent change in earth's tilt, which supposedly has changed the months in regard to horoscope signs, could affect you. Slide number 3: "Based on your dutiful reading of your horoscope, you have come to understand that you are a beacon of creativity, leadership or wisdom. Not anymore. You may instead possess qualities of thoughtfulness, intelligence or insight. Make drastic changes in your life to reflect this."

61 [http://en.wikipedia.org/wiki/Zoroaster]

62 Ibid.

63 Ibid.:

While the division along the lines of Zoroaster/astrology and Ostanes/magic is an "oversimplification, the descriptions do at least indicate what the works are *not*." They were not expressions of Zoroastrian doctrine, they were not even expressions of what the Greeks and Romans "*imagined* the doctrines of Zoroastrianism to have been." The assembled fragments do not even show noticeable commonality of outlook and teaching among the several authors who wrote under each name.

64 Frances Rolleston, *Mazzaroth or The Constellations* (London: Rivingtons, Waterloo Place, 1862) [http://philologos.org/__eb-mazzaroth]; E. W. Bullinger, *The Witness of the Stars*, 1893 [http://philologos.org/__eb-tws/]; Joseph Augustus Seiss, *The Gospel in the Stars* (New York, NY: Charles C. Cook, 1910). These three propose that the prophecies of the Gospel are to be found in the constellations and even star names. John P. Pratt, *Review of Gospel in the Stars*, ([http://www.johnpratt.com/items/docs/gis/gis_review.html], Sat 10 July 2004) is a thoughtful and useful review of this material.

65 [http://www.novareinna.com/constellation/cancer.html]

66 [http://en.wikipedia.org/wiki/Creation_myth]:

> The earth-diver is a common character in various traditional creation myths. In these stories a supreme being usually sends an animal into the primal waters to find bits of sand or mud with which to build habitable land. Some scholars interpret these myths psychologically while others interpret them cosmogonically. In both cases emphasis is placed on beginnings emanating from the depths. Earth-diver myths are common in Native American folklore but can be found among the Chukchi and Yukaghir, the Tatars and many Finno-Ugrian traditions. The pattern of distribution of these stories suggest they have a common origin in the eastern Asiatic coastal region, spreading as peoples migrated west into Siberia and east to the North American continent.

As an example, Ojibway – [http://www.gct3.net/wp-content/uploads/2008/01/creation_story.pdf]

67 Its golden fleece is the object of Jason and the Argonauts later quest.

68 Some say that Moses and the Israelites' Exodus from Egypt fits the time slot of the early second millennia BC, which really does not change much in terms of Israel's association with "the Ram" [http://oahspestandardedition.com/OSAC/Exodus11.html].

69 The root for the Hebrew "ram" has two directions, on one hand it speaks of "to be first, in front of," as the leader of the flock, however it also encompasses the concept of foolishness:

> As indicated, 'ewil primarily refers to moral perversion of insolence, to what is sinful rather than to mental stupidity. This kind of a fool despises wisdom and is impatient with discipline…Thus the fool scorns and despises restitution for the injuries and sins he commits (NIV, "Mock at making amends for sin"). He flouts his responsibility to the community as a responsible person. … [R Laird Harris, *Theological Wordbook of the Old Testament*, vol I (Chicago: Moody Press, 1981), 19].

70 If the lengths of "the Great Months" are constant (although we know that a top's wobble becomes more pronounced as the top's spin slows down, and we do not know how much a catastrophe such as a world–wide flood would affect the earth's spin), "the Age of Cancer" ("the Age of Creation") – coming before Gemini ("the Age of mankind and its Fall") and Taurus ("the Age of Noah") and Aries ("the Age of Abraham") – could have occurred about 6,480 BC (with apologies to Bishop Ussher's 4004 BC as the date of creation). Note that God does not need the full "Great Month" to accomplish creation.

71 Frances Rolleston, section: "Second Part: The Encampment Of Israel In The Wilderness (Num 2), And The Breastplate Of The High Priest."

72 In a certain irony, we are familiar with the musical *Hair*'s glorying in "the Age of Aquarius," because it seems that it will right so many wrongs with our world. Humanly speaking, Aquarius will be the "age of practical technology" and there are many claims of inventions that are "Aquarian" – although it is questionable whether this "Age" can really cop the honors for such, especially since some of these inventions began at least a

hundred years or more ago. Anyway it is the "Age" of hope, wishes, brotherhood, humanitarianism, etc. – which again really does not sound like an Aquarian invention but rather a Judeo-Christian emphasis.

But then the wonderful picture becomes a bit more sour. "Progress" is not always progress – sophistication may increase, but at what expense? This "Age" is supposed to rule the public or mass consciousness "which does not reason, but responds to life through emotions. ... The negative qualities of Aquarius include unpredictability, thoughtlessness, detachment, fanaticism and disorganization" [astrologer Dieter Koch]. It really does not sound all that different than what the world has experienced even from ancient times – although perhaps it will be more so.

73 Frances Rolleston, section: "Second Part: LIBRA The Scales, The Redeeming"

74 [http://en.wikipedia.org/wiki/Ophiuchus]

75 Frances Rolleston, section: "First Part: What Are The Real Meanings Of The Emblems Of The Signs?"

76 John Cole, *A Treatise on the Circular Zodiac of Tentyra, in Egypt* (London: Longman and Co., 1824).

77 Frances Rolleston, section: "First Part: What Are The Real Meanings Of The Emblems Of The Signs?"

78 As suggested by Rolleston, Bullinger, and Seiss (see note 64)..

79 http://en.wikipedia.org/wiki/Elul

80 For the dates of the prior triple conjunction of Jupiter and Saturn in Pisces:

May 29, 7 BC – *Sivan* 1 (*Shavot – Sivan* 6-7)
October 1, 7 BC – *Tishri* 8
November 14, 7 BC – *Heshvan* 22 - no holiday

Although the first of the conjunctions is near *Shavot*, and the second is in the middle of the celebrations at the beginning of *Tishri (Rosh HaShanah, Yom Kippur, Sukkoth)*, the third conjunction has no celebration even in the neighborhood. That sequence does not provide as interesting an array of imagery as do the conjunctions noted in the text.

81 Using the *Fourmilab Calendar Converter.*

82 Ariela Pelaia, "The High Holidays: All About the Jewish High Holidays (Holy Days)", [About.com] Guide

83 Eddie Chumney, in the thread "The Shofar: First Trump / Last Trump" in the "Hebraic Heritage Newsgroup" [http://www.hebroots.org/hebrootsarchive/9710/971009_c.html]:

Genesis 22 is the primary Torah reading for Rosh HaShanah. This is the story of Abraham going to offer his son Yitzchak (Isaac) on the altar. As he was about to do so, the angel of the Lord intervened and Abraham saw a RAM (male lamb) caught in the thicket. The ancient rabbi's saw the thicket representing the sins of the people. The two horns of the ram caught in the thicket were given a name. The left horn was called the FIRST TRUMP and the right horn was called the LAST TRUMP.

128

Therefore, the shofar (ram's horn) was seen as playing a significant role in the redemption.

The third significant shofar in the redemptive plan of God is called the GREAT TRUMP. The GREAT TRUMP is associated with and is blown on YOM KIPPUR.

[84] Martin states that although each first of the month (New Moon) is announced by the blowing of trumpets [Num.10:10], this "Last Trump" ends the Jewish festival year (the first seven months) and the sound is not heard until five months later as the festival year begins again.

[85] John J. Parsons, "Rosh Hashanah - Awakening to Judgment" [http://www.hebrew4 christians.com/Holidays/Fall_Holidays/Rosh_Hashannah/rosh_hashannah.html]:

There are four primary types of shofar blasts:

1. Tekiah … - A long single blast (the sound of the King's coronation)
2. Shevarim …. - Three short wail-like blasts (signifying repentance)
3. Teru'ah … - Nine staccato blasts of alarm (to awaken the soul)
4. Tekiah ha-Gadol … - A great long blast (for as long as you can blow!)

The general custom is to first blow tekiah, followed by shevarim, followed by teruah, and to close with tekiah hagadol

[86] *Ibid.*

[87] Martin, Chapter VI:

And note: Professor Thorley who reviewed the first edition of my work has shown that there are exactly twelve stars surrounding the head of Virgo as we see them from earth. And indeed there are. If one will look at Norton's Star Atlas, twelve visible stars will be seen around Virgo's head. They are (according to astronomical terminology): (1) Pi, (2) Nu, (3) Beta (near the ecliptic), (4) Sigma, (5) Chi, (6) Iota — these six stars form the southern hemisphere around the head of Virgo. Then there are (7) Theta, (8) Star 60, (9) Delta, (10) Star 93, (11) Beta (the 2nd magnitude star) and (12) Omicron — these last six form the northern hemisphere around the head of Virgo. All these stars are visible and could have been witnessed by observers on earth.

[88] Although the following is a tradition for *Rosh HaShanah*, actually it fits better on *Yom Kippur*. Ellen Kavanaugh, "Yom Teruah: Day Of The Shofar Blast," [http://www. lightofmashiach.org/yomteruah.html]:

There is also an interesting rabbinic tradition of Tashlich, which is the act of casting bread crumbs into a moving body of water to symbolize the removal of our sins. This comes from Micah 7:19: "He will turn again, he will have compassion upon us; he will subdue our iniquities; and thou wilt cast all their sins into the depths of the sea." Tashlich means 'to cast.'

[89] Some cultures, as do the Hebrews/Jews, count the fragment of a time unit as a whole unit. So, while we would say that a week from today is seven days away, since the Jew counts today's fragment of the day, would say a week from today is eight days away.

[90] Curiously, one might think that this would fit better following the Passover celebration (six months later), since the Passover celebrates the release from Egypt. But then it would not become one of the symbols that surround the birth of Jesus.

[91] Also Ezekiel 37:26-27; Isaiah 25:8-9; also Jesus' promise to be wherever two or three are gathered in His Name [Matthew 18:20]; also the Holy Spirit's dwelling in us [for example, I Corinthians 3:16]; also the fact of Holy Communion – all these speak not of we being with God, but that Jehovah's deepest yearning is to be *with us* .

[92] [http://www.jewishvirtuallibrary.org/jsource/Judaism/holidayc.html]:

> Shavuot is not tied to a particular calendar date, but to a counting from Passover. Because the length of the months used to be variable, determined by observation (see Jewish Calendar), and there are two new moons between Passover and Shavuot, Shavuot could occur on the 5th or 6th of Sivan. However, now that we have a mathematically determined calendar, and the months between Passover and Shavuot do not change length on the mathematical calendar, Shavuot is always on the 6th of Sivan (the 6th and 7th outside of Israel).

[93] Chapter III, C, 4, Astrology's True Mission, page 38.

[94] In his book, *Covenant: The Blood Is The Life - Tracing the River of Blood from the Tree of Knowledge to the Tree of Life*, this writer has completed an extensive survey of Covenant in the Bible and has been impressed with the power of this unique relationship built on love and grace, which lays the basis for the New Covenant through Jesus.

[95] "What is Shavuot? Re-accept the Torah" [http://www.chabad.org/library/article_cdo/aid/609663/jewish/What-is-Shavuot.htm]

[96] Bullinger, *The Witness*, pg 22.

[97] Ari Levitt [http://www.familybible.org/HolyDays/TishaB%27Av.htm]:

> Originally, the fast was observed on the Ninth of Tammuz since that was the day Jerusalem fell prior to the destruction of the First Temple in 586 BCE. However, after Jerusalem fell on the 17th of Tammuz — prior to the destruction of the Second Temple - the Sages decided upon a combined observance for both tragedies, the 17th of Tammuz.

[98] See endnote 88.

[99] The essential difference between the Biblical Testaments is that the Old Testament *has* Covenants, but in the New Testament Jesus *is* the Covenant. Covenant describes an extraordinary unity between two persons, bound by one Blood, one Life; in the Old Testament it is more conceptual and theoretical, but in Jesus, two actually do share one Blood – both God and Man are joined in one Blood, one Life.

A greater development of this theme is found in this author's book, "Covenant: The Blood Is The Life - Tracing the River of Blood from the Tree of Knowledge to the Tree of Life."

[100] Mark 6:17-20 (also Matthew 14:3-5):

> For Herod himself had sent and laid hold of John, and bound him in prison for the sake of Herodias, his brother Philip's wife; for he had married her. For John had said to Herod, "It is not lawful for you to have your brother's wife." Therefore

Herodias held it against him and wanted to kill him, but she could not; for Herod feared John, knowing that he was a just and holy man, and he protected him. And when he heard him, he did many things, and heard him gladly.

[101] This is good wisdom because 1. since she is just finishing her menstrual period, Joseph is not allowed to touch her [Leviticus 15:19-24] and she could not be impregnated yet anyway; 2. she is with Elizabeth for three months, probably until John is born, and returns home already three months pregnant, so that there is no mistake that Jesus' father is *not* Joseph

[102] Darrell Pursiful, "When Was Jesus Born? Zechariah's Priestly Service," posted on December 18, 2006 [http://pursiful.com/2006/12/when-was-jesus-born-zechariahs-priestly-service/]

[103] However Elimelech David Ha-Levi [http://www.angelfire.com/pa2/passover/jewish-calendar-hebrew.html], identifies problems even here:

> The Hebrew calendar has had three forms: (1) Biblical times: the first form, dating from the time before the destruction of the Second Temple in Jerusalem in 70 C.E. by the Romans, was a calendar based on observations; (2) Talmudic times: the second form, in effect during the Talmudic period (about 10 B.C.E. to about 500 C.E.), was based on observations and calculations; and (3) Post-Talmudic times: the third form, was based solely on calculations that defined rules for a calendar initially described in full by Moses Maimonides in 1178 C.E. ... The rules that were developed attained their final form either before 921 C.E. or before 820 C.E. However, because the modern lunisolar Hebrew calendar had to add extra months to synchronize itself with the Christian solar calendar, starting with three consecutive years that were given extra months in the 2nd century C.E. according to the Talmud, the modern Hebrew calendar cannot be used for determining Biblical dates because new moon dates may be in error up to four days and months may be in error up to four months.... In Temple times, the additional month was added periodically, after an examination of the condition of the crops I.E. the agricultural produce, at the end of the 12th month. Later on, when the 19-year cycle of the Jewish calendar was established, the extra month was added automatically, seven times in the 19-year cycle.

This does not mean that the Hebrew calendar has been chaotic – there are three anchor points for it: it is based on the moon cycles, it is connected to the solar agricultural year for its required festivals, and within the Babylonian-originated 19 year cycle, every cycle should end up where the cycle began in the solar year, therefore, with caution, generally the dates should be dependable. If we start trying to move the extra months around too much, then the correlation of sky events with Hebrew festival dates becomes futile.

[104] Edersheim, *The Life and Times of Jesus the Messiah*, Appendix vii. On the Date of the Nativity of Our Lord, note 6 - [christianbookshelf.org-edersheim-the_life_and_times_of_jesus_the_messiah-appendix_vii_on_the_date.htm]

[105] Pursiful, "Zechariah's Priestly Service."

[106] The month *Nissan* is mentioned in *Wars*, III, 1 at the beginning of the Roman siege, but without any apparent reference to the course of priests.

[107] The Moon is full, and Saturn is merrily trekking its way through Taurus, the bull – often a bull was used for a sin offering:

> You shall also have the bull brought before the tabernacle of meeting, and Aaron and his sons shall put their hands on the head of the bull. Then you shall kill the bull before the LORD, by the door of the tabernacle of meeting. You shall take some of the Blood of the bull and put it on the horns of the altar with your finger, and pour all the Blood beside the base of the altar.... But the flesh of the bull, with its skin and its offal, you shall burn with fire outside the camp. It is a sin offering.
>
> Exodus 29:10-14

> You shall offer a bull every day as a sin offering for atonement. You shall cleanse the altar when you make atonement for it, and you shall anoint it to sanctify it.
>
> Exodus 29:36

[108] http://www.mazzaroth.com/ChapterSix/TheStarOfBethlehem.htm:

> Ancient Tradition supposes that the star of Bethlehem was in the constellation Coma Berenices [a decan of Virgo] which is northwest from Virgo. That same tradition tells us that Zoroaster, the Persian religious leader, was a student of Daniel when he was in Babylon. He learned from Daniel that a star would appear in the constellation Coma when that One whom it foretold was to be born.

[109] Martin, Chapter II, subheading "The Professional Role of the Magi"

[110] [http://en.wikipedia.org/wiki/Triangulation]:

> The use of triangles to estimate distances goes back to antiquity. In the 6th century BC the Greek philosopher Thales is recorded as using similar triangles to estimate the height of the pyramids by measuring the length of their shadows at the moment when his own shadow was equal to his height; and to have estimated the distances to ships at sea as seen from a clifftop, by measuring the horizontal distance traversed by the line-of-sight for a known fall, and scaling up to the height of the whole cliff. Such techniques would have been familiar to the ancient Egyptians. Problem 57 of the Rhind papyrus, a thousand years earlier, defines the seqt or seked as the ratio of the run to the rise of a slope, i.e. the reciprocal of gradients as measured today. The slopes and angles were measured using a sighting rod that the Greeks called a dioptra, the forerunner of the Arabic alidade. A detailed contemporary collection of constructions for the determination of lengths from a distance using this instrument is known, the Dioptra of Hero of Alexandria (c. 10–70 AD), which survived in Arabic translation; but the knowledge became lost in Europe.

[111] Bullinger, *The Witness*, pg 22.

[112] A well is an important player when Erastosthenes determines the circumference of the earth with a remarkable accuracy. [http://www.mlahanas.de/Greeks/Eratosthenes.htm];
[http://www.eg.bucknell.edu/physics/astronomy/astr101/specials/eratosthenes.html]

[113] Darrell Pursiful, "When Was Jesus Born? Clement of Alexandria," December 19, 2006 [http://pursiful.com/2006/12/when-was-jesus-born-clement-of-alexandria/]:

William Tighe, however, has challenged this theory, asserting that there is in fact no evidence for a pagan observance of December 25 prior to emperor Aurelian's decree. In Rome, the principal feasts in honor of the unconquered sun took place in August, and, as Hippolytus and Julius Africanus attest, Christians had already been celebrating the date as the birthday of Jesus for at least 50 years before Aurelian. December 25 as "the birthday of the sun" is definitely pagan, but there is no evidence it is pre-Christian.

According to Tighe,

> In the Julian calendar, created in 45 B.C. under Julius Caesar, the winter solstice fell on December 25th, and it therefore seemed obvious to Jablonski and Hardouin [who first proposed the pagan connection] that the day must have had a pagan significance before it had a Christian one. But in fact, the date had no religious significance in the Roman pagan festal calendar before Aurelian's time, nor did the cult of the sun play a prominent role in Rome before him.

There may well have been syncretistic borrowing involved in the creation of a December 25 holiday, but the direction of that borrowing is largely in the opposite direction from what is normally supposed.

But isn't December 25 associated with the birth of Mithras? No, it is not. At least, Mithraic scholars seem not to be aware of this fact. The earliest existing record of the story of Mithras' birth dates from the second century, perhaps a hundred years after the Gospel accounts were written. Christopher Butler has catalogued the supposed parallels between Jesus and Mithras and finds them all wanting... Nowhere in these myths is there explicit reference to December 25 as the birthday of Mithras. The assertion that December 25 was Mithras' birthday relies on an identification of Mithras with the "unconquered sun" of Aurelian—which may or may not be a valid identification!

[114] Barry Setterfield [http://www.setterfield.org/startechnical.html] comments that the 25th Kislev and 25th December, are the same day "up until 1583 AD, the time when the Gregorian calendar was introduced." Since the Hebrew adding of the required extra months (7 months within each 19 years) goes back to Babylonian times, and the Julian and the Gregorian Calendars have longer months (not determined by the moon as the Hebrew months are) and therefore need no periodic additional month, the two calendars would only most rarely coincide.

[115] Admittedly there can be problems with the Hebrew Calendar system in terms of its relationship to the western calendars (Julian and Gregorian). If one extrapolates the cycle of 19 years back from today, there is no guarantee that somewhere especially in the first millenium AD adjustments and even disjointedness may have occurred. Suppose it was in the previous Hebrew year that the extra month was added, then *Hanukah* would indeed have come on the 22nd of December. But then the spring and summer festival dates would also all be a month later and would have no relation to what was happening in the sky. Since there really is no way to check the accuracy of the Hebrew calendar dates, it is up to the reader whether to accept, for instance, the *Fourmilab Calendar Converter* results to be as accurate as we can know.

[116] Because Luke 2:39 says, "So when they had performed all things according to the law of the Lord, they returned to Galilee, to their own city, Nazareth," some maintain that

the Holy Family immediately returns to Nazareth and only because they come down for a festival in Jerusalem do they happen to be in Bethlehem when the Magi find them. The difficulty with this scenario is, how would the Magi have found them? Going to Nazareth for x number of months and then returning would tend to lose the continuity needed for the Magi to discover the child. Also Luke says nothing about the trip to Egypt, after which Matthew tells us that Joseph decides (and is told) to turn aside to Galilee [Matthew 2:22-23]. Luke is simply skipping ahead, especially since the story of the Magi and of Egypt are already told.

117 Martin, Chapter II, subheading "The Magi Saw an Actual Star":

> Remember, this period of time was one when astrological interpretations made by first-class professionals were looked on as valid scientific indications of impending events. So confident was the Roman government about such matters, that some sixty years before, the Roman Senate ordered that all boy babies must not be allowed to live in 63 B.C.E. when astrological and prodigious forecasts had determined a "King of the Romans" was to be born. This earlier event would have been well known to Herod and to people throughout the Roman Empire. To secure its supposed validity in the opinion of people at the time, Augustus Caesar was indeed born in that very year. Herod must have felt a great deal of uneasiness when similar prognostications were being made by the Magi about a king of the Jews who had just been born.

118 Josephus, *Wars*, II, xiv, 3; VI, ix, 3.

119 *The Babylonian Talmud*, translated by Michael L. Rodkinson: "Tract Pesachim (Passover)" [http://www.sacred-texts.com/jud/t03/index.htm]:

> If the eve of Passover, however. fell on Friday, when the paschal lamb must be roasted before the Sabbath set in, the literal text of the passage in the Scriptures is abided by, and the daily offering is slaughtered as soon as the sun commences setting towards the west, i.e., half an hour after noon. ...
>
> Why should the Passover-sacrifice follow the daily offering? Because an act concerning which it is written [Deut. xvi. 6]: "There shalt thou slay the Passover (lamb) at evening, at the going down of the sun," and [Exod. xii. 6]: "They shall kill it toward evening," must be accomplished later than an act concerning which it is only written [Numb. xxviii. 4]: "Thou shalt prepare it toward evening."

120 http://www.bethlehemstar.net/

121 The reason why "(Hebrew) years" are indicated is because since the length of the Julian/Gregorian calendar does not coincide with the Hebrew year, in Julian years this date is six days too late.

122 The thought has been to use the number of Julian days between Jesus' death to the fall of Masada to extrapolate back from the destruction of the Temple to determine the beginning of Jesus' ministry, which would indicate July 28 (*Av* 10), 30 AD. However, we really have no authority to do so, since nothing in the Bible indicates even the general date when Jesus began his ministry, other than He "was about thirty," which probably was more for the sake of showing He was at an appropriately mature age rather than nailing down a definitive date.

The other method would be to try to determine from the position of the stars as to what would indicate the beginning of His ministry. This is dangerous for two reasons: 1) this can only be guesswork and cannot provide *any* reliable solution; 2) this can tread into the area of "corrupted" astrology, that is, that rather than the heavens reflecting the Story on earth as we know it, instead *it* now determines what "ought" to happen.

[123] Vexierbild by Erhard Schön

The first image shows strange landscapes with coastlines, ships and villages; looking at the picture at a low angle from the left, just off the surface of the paper, there are the portraits of Charles V, Ferdinand I, Pope Paul III and Francis I (see second picture).

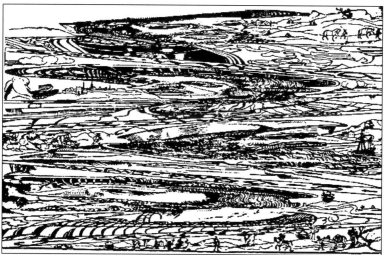